Snowboarding
BASICS

Sterling Publishing Co., Inc.
New York

This book is based on a work of the German Association
of Ski Instructors [Deutscher Verband für das Skilehrwesen]
committee on technique and methodology: Dr. Ulrich Göhner,
Chairman and Subject Editor; Florian Brunner; Sven Huckenbeck;
Volker Klinger; Ulrich Kürschner; and Tobias Blank, member of
the extended work group.

All photographs by Walter Kaiser; except for Wojciech Z., pages
12 (bottom), 33, 36, 45

Diagrams by Jörg Malr

Edited by Claire Bazinet

Library of Congress Cataloging-in-Publication Data
Lehrplan Snowboarding. English
   Snowboarding basics.
      p. cm.
   "This book is based on a work of the German Association of
Ski Instructors"—T.p. verso.
     Includes index.
     ISBN 0-8069-9623-4
     1. Snowboarding. I. Deutscher Verband für das Skilehrwesen.
II. Title.
GV857.S57L4413   1999
796.9—dc21   99-31407
                                       CIP
10 9 8 7 6 5 4 3 2 1

Published by Sterling Publishing Company, Inc.
387 Park Avenue South, New York, N.Y. 10016
Original edition published in German as *Lehrplan Snowboarding*
© 1998 BLV Verlagsgesellschaft mbH, Munich
This English edition © 1999 by Sterling Publishing Co., Inc.
Distributed in Canada by Sterling Publishing
c/o Canadian Manda Group, One Atlantic Avenue, Suite 105
Toronto, Ontario, Canada M6K 3E7
Distributed in Great Britain and Europe by Cassell PLC
Wellington House, 125 Strand, London WC2R 0BB, England
Distributed in Australia by Capricorn Link (Australia) Pty Ltd.
P.O. Box 6651, Baulkham Hills, Business Centre, NSW 2153, Australia
Printed in Hong Kong
All rights reserved

Sterling ISBN 0-8069-9623-4

Contents

Preface

The success of the German Association of Ski Instructors in putting together the snowboarding manual now mandatory for all its Deutscher Verband für das Skilehrwesen (DSV) member associations is certain to fill a long-standing gap for snowboarding associations and groups and the myriad instructors and enthusiasts around the world.

It could not have been an easy task to work out common ground upon which all the knowledgeable authors could agree and which reflects all styles of snowboarding. Yet, this team accepted the challenge and after, I'm sure, rounds of discussion, there now exists a curriculum to serve the needs not only of long-standing snowboarding instructors but those not yet familiar with the subject, as well as intrepid fledgling snowboarders themselves. Although, as with all young sports, there may be changes to be made before the "official" rules are written, if they ever can be, the experts of the DSV have here advanced the sport tremendously and, through editions of this book, will continue to play an important part in the future of snowboarding.

—Dr. Harald Kiedaisch, President, German Association of Ski Instructors

Part 1: Starting Out— Basic Goals

First
Experiences

Getting used to different forms
of movement and, in particular,
developing a sense of the board
are sure to be the beginner's first
concerns. Also important are general
safety issues and such basics as board
handling, skating on the snowboard,
maintaining balance, gliding, edging,
jumping, falling and getting up,
and riding lifts. These are all basic
elements of every beginner's class.
  It is after these first experiences
that the beginner is ready to move
on toward the next main goal—
carving turns. Skills are sharpened
as students gain experience at
this early stage, especially
in the areas of balance, gliding,
edging/sliding/stopping
and traversing.

Regular or goofy?

The first question every newcomer to snowboarding asks is "What is 'regular' and what is 'goofy,' and which group do I belong to?" meaning, "Which foot should I place in front of the other?"

A regular rider places the left foot forward, a goofy rider places the right foot forward. There is no foolproof test to tell beginners which of their feet should be placed forward. The following exercises, however, might help you to figure out which is your preferred pivot leg:

✦ Getting up from a push-up — the foot that is placed in front first is also placed forward on the snowboard.
✦ The pivot leg you use when you ride a scooter also stands in front on the snowboard.
✦ The foot in front when riding downhill on a mountain bike stands forward on the snowboard.
✦ The take-off leg for long or high jumps stands in front.
✦ Other previous experiences, like skateboarding, usually also give clues as to which leg you should be placing in front while you are snowboarding.

Soft or hard?

The second question of crucial importance to the snowboarder is "Should I get soft or hard boots?" Both types are used in the sport, but their respective bindings have different effects on the riding quality.

Before deciding on a preferred snowboarding style—freestyle, free-ride or alpine racing—every snowboarder should learn basic snowboarding techniques *in the snow*. These days, at practically every winter sports resort, you can

Always secure the board to the wrist with the leash when carrying.

rent a snowboard along with some boots and bindings. This way, you can try out both systems, and the decision on what to buy can be made later.

The combination of soft boots and bindings gives a pure "surf" feeling in deep snow, allows for maximum movement in the ankle joints for acrobatic jumps in the half pipe and all kinds of freestyle actions on the slopes. Soft bindings are comfortable to wear, but the power transmission from foot to board is not as strong as with a hard boot.

The combination of plate binding and hard-shell boot offers a more precise transmission of energy from rider to board. Using the leverage of the boot makes a dynamic as well as economical riding style possible. This combination is very good for athletic riding on the slopes. Because the ability to move is more restricted than with soft boots, hard-shell boots are not suited for half pipes.

Handling the board

The most important aspect in handling the board is safety: not to injure or endanger other winter

sport athletes due to improper handling of the board. For this reason, the board must always be carried vertically, close to one's body, and with the leash secured to the wrist.

When putting down the snowboard, it must always be laid with the bindings facing down and slightly pushed into the snow in order to prevent any sliding. When leaned against the ski rack, it must be secured with the leash so it does not fall or slide off. Never just stick the board in the snow!

Getting on the board

The board can be buckled-on while standing, with the person facing the mountain (frontside), or sitting down, with the back of the person facing the mountain (backside). It is, however, always necessary to have a secure standing or sitting position.

✦ Attach the leash to the front leg.
✦ Put the board down across the fall line. The soles of the boots must be free of snow to ensure a snug fit of the bindings.
✦ The front foot slips into the binding first, then the back foot.

Ensure a tight fit!

How to enter bindings depends on the system. There are two kinds of bindings. Plate bindings are plates that are securely anchored to the board and which can be entered wearing special hard-shell boots or ski boots. The other, soft, binding is a plastic molding with a shell bracket securely anchored to the board. Some models are equipped with a top buckle. This is a strap with a buckle that embraces the lower calf. On plate bindings with front fasteners, the boot is inserted directly into the heel clip and then the front part of the foot is locked-in by pulling down the binding lever. Be sure that the heel strap is snug, otherwise the boot may come loose during riding. Plate bindings with an automatic step-in make it

easier for you to enter the binding. Most soft bindings have ratchet straps. The straps are inserted into the locking mechanism, and most of them can be tightened using a rocker lever. A variety of easy-strap systems have been developed for soft boots, to make getting in and out of them easier.

Falling and getting up

Among the first experiences of a snowboarder is falling which, in the beginning, happens far more often than one would like. To prevent injury, it's important to practice falling correctly. If you lose control during practice, you can let yourself fall safely if you have learned how to do this.

Two techniques need to be

learned—falling frontside and falling backside. The falling techniques are first practiced without the board, and later with it.

Frontside falls

Form your hands into fists, hold your arms flexed and close to the body. First, lower the body towards the ground and then stretch out flat across the snow without touching the snow with the knees. The actual fall is mainly absorbed by the forearms.

Backside falls

Again, the arms are held close to the body, but this time more towards the side. The chin is pulled down onto the chest. Whenever you are falling, make yourself small and roll up your back and shoulders to the ground. The most important rule when falling is never to try to absorb the fall with outstretched arms!

Getting up

Because both feet are attached to the board, getting up is an act of balance. First the board has to be lined up across the fall line. Then the body's center of gravity has to be brought as close as possible to the board by propping yourself up

Falling frontside: when falling, stretch out flat in the snow

Falling backside

with the arms. Push hard with the arms to get up, bringing the front leg up first.

When facing the frontside, getting up is relatively easy. While facing the backside, on the other hand, getting up requires some practice and skill. The upper body must lean far over the tip of the board. This way, your legs are out of the way. If getting up this way is not successful, roll over to the frontside by lying on your back and lifting the board with force out of the snow. Now, roll over the shoulders to the frontside.

Skating

"Skating" on the snowboard is gliding with the front leg attached to the board while pushing yourself with the back foot, like riding a scooter. Every snowboarder must master skating in order to move over flat terrain, move in the lift line and get on and off the lift. The first step is to "walk" in a straight line or in a circle with the front foot secured in the binding. From this walking movement, you can develop to skating. The back foot pushes and is transferred to the board, onto the non-skid pad between the two bindings, during the gliding phase.

When snowboarding, it's important that the eyes always face in the direction of travel, not be focussed on the board!

Exercises:
+ walk in small "skating steps"
+ prolong gliding phases by pushing harder
+ relay games (observe safety rules!)

By using the skating technique snowboarders can acquire their first gliding experiences. Since this technique requires that the board be attached to the front leg only, the front leg may be exposed to high strain in case of a fall. It is, therefore, imperative to practice on flat, even terrain and at low speeds.

Ready position and balancing

The basic ready position is not an exactly determined, stiff position on the board. Nevertheless, it is characterized by certain attributes that serve as orientation in different situations.

The body is in a ready-to-move position so that movements are possible in all directions. Ankles, knees, and hip joints are in a slightly flexed position.

The movement axes of the body are slightly shifted on top of each other. The arms are slightly flexed in front of the body. The body weight is spread evenly onto both feet. Make sure that the posture is relaxed; this can be practiced by

Skating with eyes facing in travelling direction

bouncing slightly or jumping up and down on one spot. When both feet are attached to the board — which means that the freedom of movement is clearly restricted — your sense of balance is really challenged. Therefore, you must practice to get a feel for balance in the described basic position for the possible kinds movement: forward-backward, up-down, and to the sides. Games on an even terrain are best-suited for the practice of balance exercises.

Exercises:

✦ jump up and down with the board
✦ jump up and down in a circle
✦ pick up things from the ground
✦ relay games
✦ push the board underneath the body in front and back
✦ jumps with lifting the board off the ground
✦ jump and flex knees
✦ bounce on the frontside and the backside edges with the support of your partner
✦ alternate edging on the frontside and backside with the support of your partner
✦ balance in a flexed position on one edge
✦ bounce rhythmically on frontside and backside edges
✦ alternate rhythmic edging on the frontside and backside while standing with your partner

Gliding

At this skill-level, gliding should be practiced on a gentle slope, with a slope going up on the other side, or on a flat run-out. In order to glide, first get into the basic position. This means get ready to move, holding the ankles, knees and hip joints in a slightly flexed position, and spreading the weight evenly over the bottoms of both feet. The weight is then shifted to the front foot to stabilize the riding direction. Different movement exercises are useful to gain experience and to get a feel for gliding on the board.

Exercises:

✦ being pushed and pulled by your partner on even terrain
✦ glide, with weight shifting from front and back
✦ try to "iron" the snow with the board
✦ glide on increasingly steeper terrain with a slope going up on the other side
✦ move the body up and down while gliding
✦ try to pick up things while you are gliding
✦ move the body up and down while gliding, according to acoustical and/or optical signals

Gliding in a ready-to-move basic position

✦ bounce rhythmically while you are gliding

Edging/sliding/ stopping

Use of the edges is absolutely necessary for controlled downhill riding. Movements needed for edging or for putting the snowboard flat on the snow prepare you for making turns. Soft movements of the ankle, knee and hip joints are important to develop a feeling for the grip of the edges. Often ski boots are too stiff to enable a snowboarder to flex down in a controlled manner; this results in choppy movements.

By sliding on the board across the fall line, you can practice control skills, using the edges as needed. This is purely a balancing exercise. Flex the body slightly as you try sliding down the mountain. This is a great way to develop speed control and stopping skills.

For this exercise, a medium-steep slope with plenty of room to "run out" is the most suitable terrain. On the flat, the downhill edge might jam because there is little room for movement.

Downward falls are much more severe than falls to the uphill side; so the chosen terrain should be a practice area and not an open slope.

Exercises:

✦ even down-sliding, possibly with a partner
✦ "stair sliding" exercise, for uneven sliding
✦ edging by shifting your weight from the front foot to back foot (so you slide down like a falling leaf)
✦ edging and stopping with a partner

First sliding attempts

+ lower your speed by controlled edging
+ alternate abrupt and controlled edging, also with a partner
+ alternate sliding and stopping
+ pre-determined edging and stopping
+ forcefully stopping, and then descending by controlled force
+ edging to your instructor's or a partner's call
+ rhythmic edging and stopping
+ getting a feeling for the tension and relaxation of your muscles

There are two ways to control sliding:

1. Edge by flexing the legs, facing up-mountain (illus. **1**). Keep the board flat against the snow by raising the body in an up-down mountain direction (illus. **2**).
2. Edge by stretching the legs and body, leaning towards the mountain (illus. **3**), and put the board flat on the snow by flexing the legs and simultaneously shifting the whole body toward the downhill direction (illus. **4**).

Traversing

Traversing, in connection with sliding, enables the snowboarder to master even steeper terrain safely, and to get to specific destination points.

When traversing, sliding and edging have to be used. From the sliding motion the body weight is shifted over to the front leg. Putting the board on the edge while using the remaining sliding force causes the board to ride forward. As when skating, one's eyes should face in the direction of travel, not at one's own feet. The terrain should be the same as for the sliding exercise.

Exercises:

+ traverse with a specific destination point
+ traverse in upright and flexed position
+ ride from traversing into edging, to a full stop
+ traverse with almost no sliding
+ traverse with bouncing on one edge

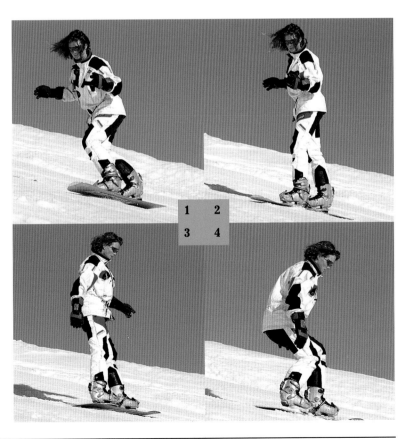

1	2
3	4

Traversing

+ explore feelings of pressure when flexing down
+ traverse using small jumps (prerequisite: finding edge and pressure point when flexing)
+ traverse using edges rhythmically
+ combine flexing down with exhaling
+ make vertical movements to acoustic signal

Hopping and jumping

Hopping and jumping are good ways to practice general readiness to move on the board. When riding over small bumps, jump up using the spring of the legs to lift the board off the ground. Flexing ankle, knee and hip joints absorbs the landing. Movement exercises using natural terrain or other means are usually quite motivating, so are a very good idea. (The motivation of students at every skill level is a topic that comes up at most instructor conferences.)

Exercises:
+ lift off at small bumps on slope
+ change from gliding to actively jumping by stretching legs and body
+ jump up in the air from a flexed body-posture at the instructor's or a partner's call
+ jump over small and medium snow bumps

Riding lifts

During the first few hours, beginners put enormous strain on their bodies because they are not yet able to move efficiently. On top of that, they often have to climb up the hill over and over. Therefore, the snowboarder should remember to take breaks once in a while. If you have a choice between a chair lift and a tow rope at a gentle slope, take the chair. The "sitting breaks" offer you a good opportunity to relax. Warning: the ability to skate in a controlled manner is absolutely necessary prior to getting on a lift.

Chair lift

To get onto the lift place the board, with the leash secured and the front foot attached to the board, in the direction of travel. Turn your upper body and watch as the chair approaches.

The leash must be securely fastened at the front foot. This is very important: If the binding should open during the lift ride, other snowboarders and skiers could be severely injured by the falling snowboard!

On chair lifts, only getting off can cause problems. In triple and quadruple chairs, beginners should sit in one of the outside positions. This way there is little or no danger that you will block other lift riders during unloading. Before getting off the lift, point the board in the direction of travel with the nose up. Put the board on the snow and, when standing up, place the back foot between the bindings. Hold onto the chair for as long as possible, then glide off to the side.

As you visit slopes, some places may allow you to ride while holding the board under the arm. If you do this, be alert to the danger: The board must absolutely be secured to the arm by the leash!

Loading at tow rope: turn upper body and grab bar

Tow-rope lift

Riding a tow rope has to be practiced with an instructor. When loading, the board points in the direction of travel and the back foot is placed on the board, pointing outward. This way you can easily turn your upper body around, look at the approaching bar and grab onto it. The bar is locked between the thighs and the back foot is placed between the bindings on the non-skid pad. The initial pulling pressure will be absorbed by the tense body posture. During the ride, more pressure is put on the front foot. Stand straight up and face and look forward. If you drift off, lean your whole body in the opposite direction and edge the board slightly. For unloading, take the bar out from between your thighs and release the bar to the front. Quickly move out and away from the unloading zone. Reattach the board in a quiet place off to the side, out of the way of others. Beginners with little experience should ride with an experienced snowboarder who can possibly iron out any unevenness in the terrain. In the event of a fall, move out of the lift line immediately. Walk to the slope with the board securely leashed.

Exercises:
- ✦ skating—ride towards someone while making eye contact
- ✦ arrange to be pulled/pushed by a partner
- ✦ simulate riding lifts by using a loose bar
- ✦ have the initial pulling pressure simulated by a partner

Unloading: release front bar and move out of unloading zone

Turns

The first "real" goal you'll encounter when learning to snowboard is to learn to make turns. Depending on your individual abilities, pre-experiences and needs, you will probably find yourself focussing more on one method of turning than another. Here, however, we will introduce you to several, using different focus points, so you can tailor your own self-instruction or better understand your instructor's directions. In the following, we'll discuss the main aspects of turning; rhythm, dynamics and balance. Understanding these aspects will help you develop your own turning technique. Most important in the implementing of these techniques, however, are the terrain and your own individual talents and preferences. Your instructor would normally base such instructions on observations of your first lessons on-site.

Snowboarding students have individual needs and previous experiences. Instructors have to be able to identify the goals and previous experiences of their students in order help them to go their individual ways. A term for this student-oriented working method could be "principle of individualization." During the first lesson, an instructor would experiment with this principle over the entire spectrum of movement to identify the scope of a "student's technique." The goal of this type of individualized teaching isn't for the instructor to teach a turning technique perfectly, but to serve as a basis which, according to the terrain and the improving abilities of the student, can be put together by the student in a meaningful manner. Learning to do turns, then, comes as a sequence of steps. These steps, or mini-goals, themselves provide important markers and can be used by the instructor, or by the student, to control the end goal—a safe turn.

Snowboarding is an outdoor sport, so conditions are not standardized. Concentrating on narrow and precise technical standards, therefore, would hinder learning. Instead, here we discuss technical "models," as background to mechanically correct movement and recurring principles of motion. Knowledge of these mechanics and their associations enables the teacher, or self-taught student, to decide what aspect of turning should be addressed next—rhythm, dynamics or balance.

There are two primary technical models, or preferred methods:
1. turns with the legs flexed
2. turns after pre-rotation

Experience has shown that most snowboarders tend to advance at a faster rate if they learn following these two technical models. Later, we will introduce a third—the turn with the legs extended.

This "open concept" of learning offers a variety of exercises so that a student, or an entire class, develops a broad "repertoire" of movements to choose from. This pool of learned motion patterns enables the snowboarder to develop a riding style that adapts to all types of terrain.

The technical model: An aid to learning

A technical model is helpful as a point of reference in solving a movement problem. It enables a student and/or a teacher to picture a certain movement without setting up every detail. Technical models, however, are usually based on ideal terrain—even, slightly to moderately steep, with packed and well-groomed snow. Any demonstrations using these "purely technical forms," therefore, are strictly for learning/teaching purposes, not as a final determination on how to strictly perform a certain technique.

Answers to the following questions prove the need for flexibility and an openness to the concept of making turns. Why does a snowboard turn and what causes it to turn?

All athletic movements are determined movements. Their mechanical correlation forms the basis for methodical actions. Basic motion patterns that, in technical models, combine the characteristics of making turns in an economical form can be broken down and identified. Typical motion patterns can be derived from the following:
1. Laws of physics
2. Motion patterns due to the physical shape of the body
3. Construction characteristics of a snowboard, including the boot-binding system
4. Solution patterns that can be helpful in certain situations

Movements are caused by the changing tensions of the muscles and result in flexing, extending or rotating motions in the participating joints. For differentiated observation of individual aspects of one complex motion, the entire motion is separated into individual motion sections (actions).

Turns with legs flexed

Technique characteristics

Turns made with the legs flexed are controlled turns on a gentle, well-groomed slope. The low body stance, caused by flexing the legs, while riding on the edge provides good balance and plenty of room for leg movement. The flexed legs also make possible the dynamic and rhythmic moves of the snowboard that are ideal for very complex steering and handling conditions.

Movement description

For traversing in medium stance, flex legs to the edge, then rise over the front leg while simultaneously leveling the board flat against the snow and rolling over to the other edge of the board by leaning into the turn. The controlled flexing of the legs allows you to steer. In brief: down for edging, up to roll onto the other edge, down to steer.

However, your goal isn't to ride a series of individual turns in a row connected by traversing, but to "connect" them with each other—to merge beginnings and ends—to ride the row of turns "cyclically." For these cyclic turns, the flexing merges first into the edging and then into the steering. This means that the movement of edging the board, prior to your rolling onto the other edge, and the movement for your steering of the board are nearly identical and don't have to be separately redone each time. The movement at the end of the first turn must be to rise over the front leg and to roll over onto the other edge, then controlled flexing and steering, and so on.

Detailed explanation

Approach: In the approach phase, you must be alert to two things: your angle to the fall line and your speed. Both must be in a range that allows the planned turn to work. On practice trails, the angle to the fall line and the terrain are pre-determined to result in an appropriate riding speed for the respective learning level.

Flexing: Flexing the ankle, knee and hip joints has two functions. First, it creates a pre-tension of the muscles for the follow-up movement of rolling onto the other edge. Second, reducing the radius at the end of a turn creates the torque necessary to lean into the new turn. This happens because of the increased edging in the flexed position from the constant leaning. It causes the flexed body, at the end of a turn, to tip over the respective edge downmountain. The edge of the board is the axis.

Rising: The rising motion that you perform when rolling onto the other edge is made up of the following components: forward—up—downward. When you are rolling onto the other edge, the previously generated torque is channeled so that your weight after rolling, caused by the "forward-movement," now shifts to the front foot. In this way, the board, when moving onto the edge again, regains the secure lead for the next turn.

The active "rising movement"—meaning the upward movement of the ankle, knee and hip joints—is actually directed downward and therefore supports the tipping of the board's edge. The "downward component," in fact, is so strong that the board, after rolling onto the other edge, depending on the speed, glides on the new edge with a slight angle.

In the technical model (under ideal conditions), the board is not rotated against the snow, but is rolled onto the other edge during the brief straightforward ride.

Turn steering: The asymmetric positioning of the feet on the snowboard challenges the snowboarding athlete's steering skills. The movements that are required for steering on frontside and backside are very different in nature.

Steering frontside: The different boot-binding systems require different ways of steering and flexing the legs.
1. In hard-shell boots, while increasing the lean into the turn, actively push the shins against the boot shaft; this serves to deliver optimal power transmission to the board. The same applies—with some restrictions—with soft bindings and top buckles. Restrictions can apply to the form and to the usual soft material inside the shells. The softer the connection, the less the power is transmitted.
2. In soft bindings, the holding forces that act against the centrifugal force have to come from the muscles only, since there's no leverage possible between shin and boot. This means that the use of the calf muscles must actively counteract the outside forces and support the ankle joints during the steering phase.

Steering backside: There are also two methods to be considered here:
1. Flexing the legs gives the knee and ankle joints a lot more room for side movement. Only

Turns with legs flexed: frontside

Turns with legs flexed: backside

after this room for movement to the sides is created can the lower leg be actively pressed forward up-mountain against the resistance of the hard-shell boot or the soft binding with top buckle. The rider feels this pressure on the outer side of the front leg and inner side of the back leg.

2. When riding with soft bindings, due to the much lower binding angles, the rider needs to make an entirely different series of moves. In bindings with toe buckles, it is necessary to master the occurring forces by sheer muscular force, by trying to retract the toes. The front shin muscle, which is affected by the retracting of the toes, is not strong enough on its own to withstand the pressure. Therefore, an increased lean into the turn must widen the edging angle. Due to the flexed legs, this movement often leads to a "sitting position." With freestyle equipment too, for as much as the binding angles allow, both knees should be pushed forward up-mountain. (Recommendation: Mount soft bindings to the

board to allow a comfortable stance, from about 20 inches (50 cm) maximum from the front and about 14 inches (35 cm) from the back. Mount them at an angle of 15 degrees.)

Legs-flexed technique

The philosophy of this method of turning is to do "turns in their entirety, right from the beginning." Therefore, at every stage in your learning, the focal point is your active movement on the snowboard. This integral method, however, also requires practicing individual movement skills. The ability to keep your balance when riding on the edge is a crucial aspect when you are learning simple and more complex moves "in their entirety." It has to be practiced separately again and again as your skills improve.

From your first lessons, the importance of flexed legs—in other words, the active flexing of the legs when riding on the edge—is paramount. The experience of turn-steering—or, more correctly, the active changing of the edging angle between board and snow

while regulating leaning—builds on that basic skill. Without this skill, a complex action is bound to fail.

If there are problems practicing the combined moves, you must address the individual problem areas and practice them separately. For beginners, practicing these on the fall line on steeper slopes is not recommended. Here, you should only practice the various maneuvers and work on riding on the edge.

Leaving the fall line

By leaving the fall line, you learn to control your speed. This challenges your balancing skills. Practicing side sliding and intense traversing prepares you to add the skill of being able to adjust your leaning. In this way you learn, from the beginning, to use the curve of the snowboard. During gliding, the legs are flexed and the body weight is shifted to one edge. (Naturally, this has to be practiced on both sides.) By your flexing of the legs, the edging angle widens and the board rides along its prescribed radius on the edge.

Leaving the fall line

Exercises:

- ✦ move from traversing into edging, by flexing down and ride until stopping
- ✦ do "fan" turns (allow yourself to slide into the fall line, then edge again and ride until stopping)
- ✦ make turns toward the mountain, leaving the fall line, until you stop

Additional training goals:

- ✦ to work out the feel of pressure on the shaft of the boot (only possible with hard-shell boots or soft bindings that have a top buckle)
- ✦ demonstrate the difference between soft and hard edging
- ✦ leaning variations during turn steering

Preparation tasks:

- ✦ rise over the front leg in a standing position until the board starts sliding downward.

Exercises:

- ✦ try to push the board flat against the snow
- ✦ stand on the ball of the foot so that the heel is lifted up

Garland

A turn garland is the result of combining "leaving the fall line" and "drifting into the fall line" moves. Riding on one edge is supplemented by actions that prepare the significant characteristics of the snowboarding technique, such as flexing the legs to steer and rising over the front foot to roll onto the other edge. This training exercise allows you to practice the leaning position when riding "actively" on the edge and prepares you for movement in the forward–rise–downward direction in order to roll onto the other edge.

Garlands can consist of different practice exercises:

- ✦ ride a rhythmic garland: traverse ride with multiple lifts of edges, but without rolling onto the other edge or drifting too far into the fall line
- ✦ garland with focus point: to improve the steering quality
- ✦ garland with focus point: to rise over the front leg
- ✦ garland with small jumps

For beginners, it's important to choose the right terrain on which to practice such integral tasks. Choose a gentle slope, perhaps one with a counter slope; that is, going up on the opposite side. The incline of the slope should be only enough so you don't gain speed when riding near the fall line. You don't want, under any circumstances, to be forced by the

Drifting into the fall line: the board needs time

Drifting into the fall line (preparing to roll onto other edge)

This exercise mainly practices the vertical movement. To drift into the fall line the body rises over the front leg in a forward-rise-downward direction—forward to secure control over the board; rise to take on a good position for the following flexing; and downward to keep the board flat on the snow. The functions of the individual components will be described in detail in the section "Extending Skills."

**Turn garland
when riding
on one edge**

**Edging
in flex**

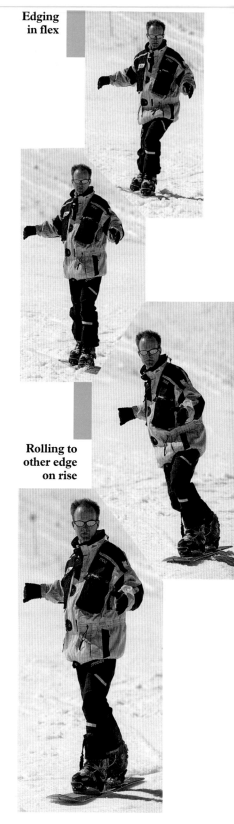

**Rolling to
other edge
on rise**

movement from one edge of
the board to the other. At first,
a beginner will not work very
intensely with the legs, but as
training continues the up-
down motion will increase. The
goal is not to actually carve turns,
but to work out an intense feel for
the rolling from one edge to the
other as well as to develop
dynamic muscle tension and
relaxation.

Preparation tasks:

✦ bounce rhythmically when
   riding the fall line
✦ bounce rhythmically with both
   legs during traversing to control
   center position
✦ rhythmic "garland," quick rising
   and controlled flexing on one
   edge—but practice both sides!
✦ exercise in standing position
   with a partner: rhythmic rolling
   with clearly visible edging angle

Exercises:

✦ follow a pre-assigned rhythm
   using a slalom course… and
   then change it!
✦ sensitize yourself, or your
   student, to notice tensions
✦ change rhythms on the called-
   out signals of your instructor or
   partner
✦ ride in pairs with same rhythm
✦ increase the dynamic all the
   way to jumping from one edge
   to the other

incline to brake. The incline of the
slope may be increased as your
skills improve, depending on the
respective exercise.

Rhythmic rolling to other edge close to fall line

Accomplishing this task requires a
beginner's thorough concentration
and preparation. Proper leg movement is very important. The goal
here is a determined and dynamic
"rolling" from one edge to the
other. The body weight has to be
shifted using a rhythmic up-down

Rhythmic rolling with wider turning angle

The vertical movement now requires a rhythmic change and has to be prolonged during the flexing. Consciously saying to yourself out loud "up−d-o-w-n, up−d-o-w-n," helps in practicing this particular task. Later it is possible to change the rhythm by moving to a different terrain. A steeper slope requires more breaking to avoid gaining too much speed. This way the task is pre-set by the terrain. If the slope is too steep, you'll need additional movements to keep the speed consistent. Pre-rotation of the torso and/or counter-rotating are successful ways to do this.

On slightly steeper terrain the flexing movement is prolonged

More useful at this stage of the learning process are other preparation tasks which you can do while riding on one edge.

Preparation tasks:
✦ practice the training goal in a standing position
✦ ride in the fall line with vertical movement, without rolling onto the other edge. Rhythm: up−d-o-w-n
✦ bounce rhythmically on one edge during the traverse; focus now on controlled flexing
✦ do garland turns
✦ make turns in uphill direction
✦ ride subsequent individual turns with movement breaks in the traverse

Additional training goals:
✦ to connect flexing with exhaling
✦ to jump over the fall line while simultaneously rolling onto the other edge, to end-jump in turn

Rhythmic rolling with increased steering quality

The focal point of this phase is the flexing of the legs specifically for steering. Exact edging and a tall-standing leaning position are necessary to improve steering quality. For this, you will need increased confidence in riding on the edge. This particular goal requires a bit more patience from instructors and beginners as well, since regulating your balance on the edge will take time and effort to work out. On steeper terrain a student has more room to vary the edging angle.

Exercises:
✦ garland with focus on improvement of steering quality
✦ turn mountainside on markings
✦ visual task: cut the slope open, ride as if on tracks
✦ ride individual turns while you keep your focus on improving steering quality
✦ set different focal points in the dynamics: up−d-o-w-n, or up−down
✦ work on an easy slalom course
✦ maintain a rhythm, then change the rhythm

Riding on the
edge is the
main concern

Rhythmic turns with increasing curve radius

Prolonging the flexing movement is the biggest problem for most beginners. Now you have to make the radius of the turn flexible, so you are able to adjust the track line to the respective terrain. The flow of movement that you learned in order to make rhythmic turns still has to be maintained. The focus now, however, is on the actual turning action.

Exercises:
✦ stay in line with a partner
✦ connect the longer radii with your breathing; inhale briefly when rolling onto the other edge, exhale long (with sound) when steering
✦ practice on the slalom course, where markers are placed farther away from the fall line

Turns after pre-rotation

Technique characteristics

Turns with a pre-rotation are drifted and controlled turns on a gentle, well-groomed slope. Torso and hip are pre-rotated in the direction of the turn. This pre-rotation effectively supports the active initiation and steering of the turns.

Movement description

The approach is a short traverse ride. Ankle, knee and hip joints are slightly flexed. The posture is relaxed, the weight equally balanced on both legs. At the beginning of the turn, torso and hip are pre-rotated in the direction of the turn and the weight is shifted more onto the front leg and inward. When the board is flat on the snow, the torso rotation is completed and is transferred to the legs and board. When at last the fall line is reached, the board is rolled onto the other edge, due to the weight shift, and into the new direction of the intended turn. Then, with evenly spread pressure on the inside edge, the turn is steered.

Detailed explanation

To effectively transfer rotation movements onto the snowboard, the torso and hip have to pre-rotate while the board is still on edge. When releasing pressure from the edge, the gained angular momentum can then be transmitted directly to the board. Depending on the intended change of direction (and the steering quality), rotation speed and intensity will need to be adjusted.

The speed of the body rotation directly influences the radius of the curve. Fast rotations cause short radii and slow rotations long radii. The intensity of the body rotation significantly influences the angle of the turn — how much the board turns in the new direction. In other words: a strong rotation will result in a significant change in the direction of the board and a slight rotation will result in a slight change of the direction.

The greater the intensity and speed of the pre-rotation motion, the easier it is to induce a turn and, therefore, to cross the fall line. Too much pre-rotation can cause problems in steering the turn because the rotation will need to be slowed down further to prevent the board from over-rotating. To increase steering quality, the pre-rotation must be controlled.

Another point affecting the steering quality is the timing between edging and pre-rotation. For drifted turns, the torso and hip are significantly pre-rotated and then the board is rolled onto the other edge.

From its narrow appearance, beginners looking at a board for the first time get the impression that it isn't easy to handle and control. At this early stage, the mechanical characteristics of the board don't yet relate to the natural forces involved in snowboarding and aren't recognized as being of constant quantity. Learning the mechanics of board use, therefore, is often neglected at this skill level. Once the board's mechanical properties become background knowledge, through experience, you will find yourself better able to exploit your board's very individual characteristics. For now, it's important for you to get the feeling of controlling the turns by rotating the body.

Technique after pre-rotation

Eliminating all disruptive factors — a slope that's obstructed, too narrow, too crowded, or too steep — is a necessity to developing a trust in the absolute controllability of the equipment. It's therefore crucial for successful practice sessions. Find a gentle slope with a long runout that will guarantee actual safety and make for psychologically important, at this stage, anxiety-free practice sessions.

There are two methods to working out the technical model and these, depending on the terrain and your skills, can be used either alternately or to supplement each other. Both methods lead to the goal, the first in an integral way, through the use of rhythm, and the second through a partly methodological manner of steering. The first method is similar to the technique that was introduced earlier, in the section on turns with legs flexed, which focussed on rolling onto the other edge close to the fall line (see page 15). This method will, therefore, not be discussed again here. Instead, we'll introduce you to the second method of working out the after pre-rotation technique model.

Actually, the partly methodological structure of the learning steps in this technique is not very challenging for beginners. In fact, if you are feeling a little bit afraid, or may be physically weaker, this way of learning is ideal for you. The technical challenge for the rider is to attune the edging with the turning angle of the board and with the scope of the pre-rotation movement of the torso.

In this method, the turns are driven irregularly and therefore leave room for controlling the general appearance of the tracks. You learn the technique by simply making mountainside turns with different approach angles (with respect to the fall line). Be sure that you practice both frontside and backside turns equally.

In the beginning, an open slope with packed snow is important. Later on, the slope should be steep enough so that turns with sufficient speed can be carried out dynamically. Finding a wide slope with various inclinations and enough run-out space is needed if you want to plan out for yourself a varied practice program with increasing challenges.

To summarize, the guidelines for learning methodological-action turns are: from traversing to steering, then steering after pre-rotation and, finally, dynamic turns after pre-rotation.

From traversing to steering

During the steering phase, a firm grip of the edges over the entire length of the board is realized by putting weight on both legs. This also prevents a slipping or over-rotation of the board. The snowboarder edges the board by pointing the knee mountainside and, because of the curve of the board, riding the board facing the mountain to a full stop. The track marks may very well look like carved steering (clear, narrow edge marks).

Note: For snowboards with little curve (such as freestyle or long, alpine race boards), it's important that the slope be wide enough and not too steep, since those boards drive a very wide curve radius even when the edging angle is steep.

Exercises:
- in standing position, tilt the board along its vertical axis
- slide with a lot of "play in the knees." (Practice: "edge: knee points *to* the mountain; relax: knee points *down* the mountain.")
- traverse with clearly visible edging

Steering mountainside after pre-rotation

After getting a feeling for steering and working out and gaining trust in the edge grip, comes learning controlled steering at drifted turns with narrow radii (according to the principle of steering after pre-rotation of the torso).

Now that you are comfortable with traversing, make your approach and rotate your torso in the mountainside direction without changing the edging angle. The result is that the rotation is transferred to the legs and the board turns in a narrower radius than before.

For the exercise to be more demanding, the approach can be made steeper or brought closer to the fall line. In this way, you can customize your learning. You can also use a steeper slope. But, to start out, and in order to overcome any fears, choose a gentle slope with plenty of run-out.

Exercises:
- from riding the fall line, make a turn towards the mountain after rotation of the torso
- turn fan (this means to ride several turns towards the mountain with increasingly steeper approaches)
- ride a turn around a marking, or around your partner, all the while keeping eye contact
- ride a turn towards the mountain to an acoustic signal
- ride a turn garland (this means to ride several turns in a row towards the mountain)
- garland with different radii
- turns toward the mountain with vertical movement: the board turns when stretching legs (this approach posture is clearly more flexed than the ready position) or flexing legs (approach posture is ready position)
- experiment with various weight shifts during turning (front/back foot)
- turn and leave the fall line again
- ride turns around a partner without a board, and help with one hand
- line up a series of turns of different radii, in different terrain and snow conditions

Additional training goals:
- when the torso is rotated against the intended direction of the turn (and the spine is therefore under unnecessary stress), the arms can be pointed in the direction of the intended turn

Steering mountainside after pre-rotation

Dynamic turns

- ✦ if the board "grabs," caused by too much edging, practice edging in a controlled manner at the initiation of the turn
- ✦ if the blade becomes buried in the snow, perhaps even coming to a stop, there is too much weight on the front leg

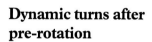

Dynamic turns after pre-rotation

At turn initiation, the combination of rotation and pressure on the front leg lets the board turn more easily on a wider blade. The back part of the board is relieved and can turn freely. Putting together such supporting means as "pre-rotation" and "pressure on the front," will result, especially in steeper terrain, in a flawless turn and crossing of the fall line. In the steering phase, a secure grip

of the edges over the entire length of the board is achieved, and sliding or over-rotating is prevented by putting your weight evenly on both legs.

Exercises:
- ✦ experiment with weight shifts during turns (front/back foot)
- ✦ in a standing position, practice the rotation movement of the torso by shifting your weight at the same time
- ✦ fan turn in relation to the fall line (this means ride several turns towards the mountain with increasingly steeper ap

proaches); during the approach, shift your weight immediately to the front, then quickly withdraw

+ ride series of turns with different radii
+ exaggerate the weight shifts
+ ride turns with your weight on the front foot to discover how quickly the board over-rotates
+ ride turns by putting weight only on the back foot. Result: the board hardly turns
+ practice in different terrains and snow conditions

Additional training goals:

+ when the board hardly turns because you have too much weight on the back foot at turn initiation, practice consciously putting your weight on the front foot
+ when the board is edged too much prior to the fall line (there is a tendency of the rider to fall inward), pay special attention to controlling the edging at turn initiation
+ to prevent the board from over-rotating at the end of the turn, give special attention to an even shifting of weight

Note: Especially at the start, don't practice on a slope that is too steep. A gentle slope is sufficient. As you initiate a turn, move forward first and then rotate, so you will feel the effect of the weight shift more distinctly and crossing the fall line will be easier. Then, do the movements simultaneously for a quicker turn initiation and asmoother, sportier ride, with narrower radii possible. Choose wider radii and put significantly more pressure on the back leg after you roll onto the other edge; at the same time, continue edging to experience the smooth and confident running caused by this "trim" over the back leg.

Steering a turn—an observation in detail

When steering, the snowboarder is actually making turns. He or she is able to vary the curve radius over the entire course of the turn by changing the edging angle between the board and the snow and, at the same time, leaning into the turn. The wider the edging angle of the board in the respective curve-leaning position, the smaller the radius of the turn. In accordance with skill level, mastering the steering of a turn is absolutely necessary for general safety. The steering quality is measured by how much the board slips or drifts in a turn. The less drifting, the better the quality. The different steering qualities are called drifted, edged and carved, in order of descending amount of slippage. The carved turn steering is the highest steering quality—only a line can be seen in the snow (see the later section on "Carving").

What makes good turn steering? During the course of the turn the snowboarder is affected by constantly changing outside forces. In addition, the snowboarder is only in equilibrium when the sum of all outside forces runs from the body's center of gravity through the supporting surface. But when turning, the board stands on its edge, and the supporting surface is just a line! It is only natural that the question of what mechanism regulates equilibrium should arise. Similar to a snowboarder standing on the slope with the board, a bicyclist standing up on a bike can keep balance only when making an effort. If the body's center of gravity has moved off-balance, there is nothing the person can do; the forces driving him away from the stable position grow with increasing distance from the balanced position. In mechanics, a balanced position like this is called an unstable equilibrium. When riding, it is a little bit easier for the bicyclist than the snowboarder. If a bike is tilted a little bit too much to the inside in a curve, a rider can gain equilibrium again by steering with the handlebars to narrow the turn a little. In this situation he is only using the centrifugal force that increases with a narrowing turn radius to return his body to balance. The snowboarder behaves in a very similar way when carving a turn. If his body's center of gravity during a turn, for example, moves to the inside and therefore out of equilibrium, he can use the curve of the board, and by widening of the edging angle achieve a narrower turn radius. This action can be used to regain balance, like in the example with the bicyclist. In this context, with a constant center of gravity, only the flexibility of the ankle joints enables a permanent regulation of the equilibrium. In constantly changing terrain and snow it is only possible to keep balanced if the turn radius is permanently adjusted. A certain flexibility in the joint of the snowboard boot is absolutely necessary to steer a turn.

If the turn steering is drifted or edged, the situation is different. Here the snowboard rider has to try to adjust the breaking skid-effect of the board by changing the edging angle. This typically results in a stuttering riding style, which is very commonly observed in beginners. Here the inner forces are almost exclusively responsible for keeping up the unstable equilibrium. The board is drifted sideways and, by flexibility in the knees, edged to various extents.

Turns with legs extended (another technical model)

Technique characteristics

In addition to turns with the legs flexed and turns after pre-rotation, there is another technical model for turns that we want to acquaint you with here: turn with the legs extended. This model is especially important to know when you are riding in deep powder and on moguls. For that reason, however, it is not necessary to learn this third technical model as early on as the other two.

Movement description

Traversing in medium stance, roll onto the other edge by rising mountainside with increased edging, then flex over the front leg, while simultaneously leveling the board flat on the snow, and roll onto the other edge by taking a curve-leaning position.

As soon as the new edge grips, use a controlled extension of the whole body straight from the edge out over the snow to steer. In brief, up to edge—down to roll onto the

other edge—up to steer. Here, too, the end of the rising motion into edging is the same as the end of the steering motion. A dynamic, rhythmic switch between muscle tension and relaxation is created by rolling to the other edge and steering.

Detailed explanation

Approach: The characteristics of the approach for this technical model are identical to that for turns with flexed legs.

Rising: By extending ankle, knee and hip joints with an increased leaning position, muscle tension builds up. This rising motion is similar to raising one's arm.

Flexing: The direction of the flexing motion is forward—down —downward. Flexing of the ankle, knee and hip joints causes the tension noted by active rising with increasing leaning position. The centrifugal force drives the body down the mountain.

Since the edge of the board in the snow serves as an opposing medium, the body is tipped downward to roll onto the other edge. The rotation axis is the vertical axis of the board. Here, the body's center of gravity is shifted downward and projected onto the new edge where balance is regained. The forward motion is based on the same technique as turning with the legs flexed. Having the body positioned low at the end of the movement rolling onto the other edge is important to the steering phase that follows.

Turn steering: By extending the legs (ankle, knee and hip joints), an increased edging angle between board and snow is further widened. Once the legs are extended, the curve radius can only be narrowed by more leaning, it cannot be widened. An actual steering motion is no longer possible. Therefore, a controlled rising motion is necessary during the entire duration of the turn.

Being able to sense the grip of the edge after rolling onto the other edge is very important. If the legs are extended before the edge grips firmly, or if they are extended too quickly, it is no longer possible to steer effectively until the turn is completed.

Steering frontside: The weight is evenly spread on both feet. The body is extended from all joints at the same time and evenly spread throughout the turn.

Steering backside: The rising of the entire body on the backside is the same as on the frontside, but is initiated by actively raising the heels.

Tips:
Stay in the flexed position until the edge grips, then extend the body dynamically in the direction of the center of the turn. For this technical model, the radii should not be too wide; your weight should be placed on the front leg.

This methodical pattern is identical to turning with the legs flexed, with the direction of the respective motions opposite, of course. "Flex to steer" is changed to "rise to steer," and "moving up to roll onto the other edge" changes to "moving down to roll onto the other edge." Tasks with jumping motion are, however, not possible.

The methodology described earlier, using these new technical models, opens up to you a variety of solutions for snowboarding in different terrain situations. The goal is a versatile pool of such models that can be varied in accordance to the respective situation.

Alternative methods

Beginners who have had no previous experience with glide-sports may find their learning of snowboarding slower than that of experienced skiers, surfers, in-line skaters or skateboard riders. That, should come as no surprise. Still, some total beginners should be able to ride down gentle slopes after only a few practice sessions. Others may, however, find themselves continuing to have balance problems. If this is the case, trying one of these alternative methods might help accelerate the learning process.

Big foots

Playful learning is the primary consideration with this "sports apparatus." At many winter sports resorts "big foots" are now

standard equipment at the rental stations. They can be fitted to any snowboard or ski boot. These easy-to-handle gliders make "playful experimenting" with all movement characteristics important in snowboarding an easy task. The first experiences and patterns that are practiced with this equipment, for turns with the legs flexed, can be translated almost entirely for use in snowboarding, and are quite successful in maximizing learning. It's an especially good way for a family or friendly group of beginners—budding enthusiasts —to get into the snowboarding experience. Exercises balancing on one leg on the inner edge of the outward-pointing leg in a turn serve as special balance training at a more advanced stage.

Tandem board

Riding on a tandem board is a pure snowboarding experience for beginners. The riders stand one behind the other on the board.

When riding with a beginner, an instructor stands in front. Due to the close body contact with a teacher or experienced rider, such specific elements as positioning, amplitude and dynamics can be directly experienced by the beginning student. While riding down a slope, various steering qualities as well as tactical elements are clearly communicated. Insecure beginners, especially, gain confidence in the overall movement pattern and are thus better able to transfer those shared experiences to their own training.

The tandem board is not meant to guide a beginner through entire methodologies, but it is helpful to communicate bodily experiences in their entirety for a better understanding. For this purpose, there's no harm in making arrangements to "hitch a ride" if you can.

The direct communication of body experiences made possible by riding the tandem board is also very well suited to accommodating a beginner who is blind. The interplay with forces and motions means emotionally experiencing a fascinating glidesport in its purest form.

The disadvantage of the tandem board method is that only one beginner at a time—per board—has the opportunity to enjoy this manner of snowboarding.

Extending Skills and Use of Tools

With the help of the learning steps so far introduced, it is possible that you have learned how to make turns. If you've arrived at this point in your training, in fact, those turns should be fairly good in general, but they are very likely characterized by an inattention to detail.

The following is dedicated to providing you with some "special" activities, the type instructors might use in order to polish their students' techniques. We'll try, here, to make clear what these

activities are expected to bring about so you can use the individual actions appropriately. This means consciously riding a turn faster, narrower, or initiating it sooner or later; mastering a turn even if the snow or the terrain is not optimal; and preparing for the advanced training section of this book, where you will learn about riding moguls, in deep powder, on steep slopes, or in difficult snow.

What can you, as an individual, do to better your performance on the snowboard and how can you put those techniques into action? The answer is simple: We'll look more deeply into those technical models for ways that have been, so far, more or less hidden and have therefore not yet been practiced. They can be used like tools to adjust movements and to solve certain problems you may have. The tools, which we'll cover in turn, include:

+ Body rotations (along the vertical axis of the body)
+ Vertical movements (up-and-down movements)
+ Weight shifts (towards the tip or the heel of the board)
+ Curve leanings and edging

Body rotations

As is commonly known, by activating different body parts we can carry out a variety of movements. A simple "rotation of the torso against the legs" may become of special importance when on a snowboard. If used properly, it can deliver an angular momentum that can be transferred to the board and used in turning.

What does "used properly" mean? To explain this restriction—theoretically—we are going to use a turning plate; that is, a disc rotating around a vertical axis. Imagine standing on the plate so

that the vertical axis of the body matches the axis of the plate. (Less spectacular and not as useful is standing on a beach towel.) If you now try to put your torso in a rotating motion, this is possible only briefly. The legs rotate (reactively) in the opposite direction as far as you can twist your body. This is commonly called "counter-rotation": hip and torso rotate in one direction; legs, and with them the plate (or the beach towel), in the other direction. Say you do the same test a second time—try to put hips and torso in a rotating motion in the same manner—but this time you have the plate held in place by a second person (or any other breaking mechanism). At the end of the test, when the plate is released, the result is that plate and the body of the test person turn in the initial rotating direction. In this case the rotation of the body is called—in accordance with the occurrence—"pre-rotation."

Both rotating motions deliver the means that enable the board to turn. Both have their special characteristics, which can be put to work to serve a certain purpose only after being practiced (like any tool).

What was described here using the example of the turning plate shall now be practiced in reality with the snowboard.

Pre- and counter-rotation tasks and exercises:

+ stand on a hilltop and put torso in rotation motion. When the board is flat on the snow, this always results in a counter-rotation.
+ jump up in the air on flat terrain and turn hip and torso *only* while airborne. When landing, the counter-rotation of the board is recognizable

- jump up in the air on flat terrain, but this time start turning hip and torso when jumping. When landing, the board will have rotated farther
- ride on flat terrain on the fall line and try to repeat the above exercises
- use different strengths of body rotation while traversing or drifting sideways to observe the results on the rotating motion on the board

Caution:

Over-rotation is a rotation that continues past a certain goal (and therefore must be corrected). When you are making turns, you don't want to drift (in other words, don't want the board to stand up across the direction of travel). The board can over-rotate very easily. This happens when, for example, your body has too much (rotation) momentum from pre-rotating. It also occurs when counter-rotating—as when you have worked-in too much counter-rotation during side-slipping. Both occurrences can, however, be prevented but you must pay close attention to maintaining controlled body rotation.

Vertical movements

Vertical movements, like the flexing and extending of the ankle, knee and hip joints, are found in almost every daily physical activity. In general, they have very determined functions. These functions can only be realized if the flexing/extending movements are administered in a certain way. (A 7-foot man bends down to get through a door without banging his head. A ski jumper flexes during the approach to minimize wind resistance and get into a good starting position for take-off. A weightlifter crouches at the end of the first lift-up as fast and as far down as possible because this is the only way for him to get *underneath* the weight in order to lift it all the way up. You can easily think of other examples.)

When snowboarding, too, you need to combine up-and-down movements (or down-and-up movements) with certain functions, which can only be realized if the vertical movement is done in a particular way. The functions of these movements are called mechanical relieving and loading.

What does this mean? If we are standing up, we "put weight" on the ground on which we are standing. If we place a newspaper between the floor and the shoes we are wearing, we wouldn't be able to pull the newspaper out from underneath our feet due to this weight. This applies to any such situation, whether we are crouching or standing straight. But when we are *moving* upward or downward, the load ratios are different for a very brief period of time. It's easier to understand an up-motion being so fast that you lift off the ground. The result, even if only for an instant, is a complete relief of the weight (the newspaper could be taken away with no problem).

Some such relief, though not completely, occurs if you move upward without actually jumping. The duration and intensity of the relief, which is also called "load relief," depend on how fast you are moving upward. Relief also, however, occurs on a movement downward. A total relief is reached when you briefly allow yourself to fall completely. On the other hand, there is very little such relief when you are moving downward slowly.

In both cases, it has to be noted that *relief is always combined with load*; relief alone does not exist. It is load that results in an increase of pressure on the ground. Therefore:

Up movement =
　　load, then relief
Down movement =
　　relief, then load
Down-up combo movement =
　　relief–load–relief
Up-down combo movement =
　　load–relief–load

What good are loading and relief in snowboarding? What functions do they serve?

Loading is used to press (carve) the edge of the board in the snow by pressure increase. Relief can be used (but doesn't have to be) to rotate the board out of its travelling direction against the (now not so strong) resistance of the snow, but also, subsequently, to put on more or less load.

How dynamic is the vertical movement supposed to be? The dynamic is determined by the functions mentioned above. A faster flexing movement farther down, for example, results in pushing the edge harder against the snow.

Tasks and exercises:
- ride in deliberately flexed and extended position
- turn rolling onto the other edge by jumping
- jump up from a flexed position
- turn with (possibly exaggerated) vertical draw-back movement
- turn or try to turn without any vertical movement
- ride a longer ride in deliberately flexed position, without ever rising

Weight shifts

Usually, almost in reflex when first getting on a board, most beginners put more load on the back leg than the front leg. This is not good, because it makes it more difficult to steer the board. As practice time on the board increases, however, riders learn to move more of their weight towards the front, so that both legs are at least equally loaded.

Later on, you will need to become sensitive and flexible with regard to loading. It's important, now, to learn to consciously shift your weight during a turn.

Shifting your weight serves several functions: If the weight is shifted onto the front leg during traversing, the board will drift into the fall line according to the spreading of the weight. The same applies if the weight is shifted towards the front of the board at the end of one turn and at the initiation of the next turn.

The weight shift towards the front of the board at the initiation of a turn is also useful if you want to make the heel of the board turn more easily (by taking load off).

In mid-curve, the edge pressure can be improved by putting your weight on the middle of the board (increased curving of the board).

Towards the end of the turn, you can let the board "run" by shifting weight more towards the back leg and therefore taking off the skid-effect of the blade pressure.

Following these two basic rules is essential:
1. More weight is put on the front leg at turn initiation.
2. More weight is put on the back leg when steering.

(When executed in a standing position, this shifting back and forth is similar to "swinging.")

Tasks and exercises:
+ ride and make turns in extreme forward- and backward-leaning positions
+ ride in a constant medium position while swinging
+ ride and make turns with a distinctive amount of swinging

Curve leanings and edging

Riding curves on a bicycle, motorcycle, skis or skates is possible because riders can produce forces that enable them to change travelling directions. In the examples above, the forces grip at the connecting point between equipment and ground or, in the case of snowboarding, between board and slope. There (and only there) does the rider have the ability to initiate the turn. (In mechanics this is called "pulling into the center of the curve"—centripetal force—and this pulling results, in the above mentioned cases, from underneath.) Because the forces don't take effect in the same way (pulling inward) at the upper portion of the body, those remain in the same state of motion (law of inertia). This would inevitably lead to a fall, if it were not possible to compensate.

In order to master a turn, a snowboarder (as well as a bicyclist, motorcyclist or skier) always has to solve two problems: Producing inward-pointing forces at the connection with the ground and, at the same time, shifting body weight by leaning into the curve.

There is a close relationship between these two activities: The more inward-pointing forces are produced, the more intense the leaning has to be.

But—especially when it comes to snowboarding—this matter can be seen differently. You can lean before the actual turn but, in order not to fall, you must also supply the respective strong inward-pointing forces later. Again, the following applies: The more you lean into a curve, the higher you will need the inward-pointing forces to be. And, if you cannot supply those needed forces, you will surely find yourself taking a spill into the snow.

After your first experiences in riding curves, it's important to explore more into the tools that are used to produce the inward-pointing forces, or the ones that are used to compensate the outward-pointing forces. The tool for inward-pointing forces is edging. When riding frontside, you can edge with the help of your knee movement, ankle joint work and by putting your weight on the ball of the foot (ball pressure); when riding backside, this is done by knee movement, ankle joint work and by putting weight on the heel of the foot (heel pressure).

Serving as tool to vary leaning in a curve, certain body positions are used. The many variations of these two possibilities (curve leaning and edging) can be practiced by doing exercises in a standing position, but mostly by exercises on traversing, drifting, turns towards the mountain, and turn fans. The turns can be customized and perfected by changing radii and speed.

**Part 2:
Advanced
Training—
Special
Goals**

Moguls

A mogul field is one of the most challenging terrains for a snowboarder. The constantly-changing sizes, forms and distances of the moguls and gaps demand a snowboarder's highest skill level. Riding moguls "forces" the rider into a certain rhythm to which he must adapt by choosing a suitable technique and riding line. To confidently and successfully master moguls requires substantial technical and tactical skills.

The individual's actions on the moguls are determined by such outside factors as inclination of the slope, size and distance of the moguls from one another, snow roughness/smoothness, and riding speed. As a technical model, the *equalization technique* applies. Equalized leg movements during the turns characterize this technique, which works best if you follow the technical model of turns with the legs flexed.

Technical model

The mogul is approached in a ready-to-move medium stance. When riding onto the mogul the legs are flexed and the board is rolled onto the other edge. This flexing of the legs is supposed to "swallow" the mogul. The turn is controlled by extending the legs in the direction of the mogul hollow and simultaneously edging the board. While riding moguls you should not rise up all the way. You need to remain in a flexed ready-to-move stance. During the entire duration of the ride, the board should just touch the snow and the upper body remain calm.

Notes and explanations

If the mogul distances are far, or if the moguls are especially high, the riding line can be changed. In such a situation it's recommended that you just ride over the "flanks" of the moguls. Rolling onto the other edge is done in-between the moguls. In gentle to medium-steep terrain, with low moguls that are far from each other, it's possible to choose a riding line exclusively in the hollows of the moguls. Here, the technical model for turns with legs flexed should be applied, with the body kept in an overall flexed position. You should stay close to the fall line when riding down the moguls because traversing in-between the moguls disrupts the flow and rhythm of the ride. The riding speed should be adapted to the rapidity of the terrain. The steeper the terrain, the lower the speed and the wider the turn angles. On gentler moguls, narrower turn angles and higher speeds are possible.

Important:

The continuous use of only one technical model is only possible if mogul fields are typically ideal. Your technique, riding line and rhythm are pre-determined by the terrain. Most of the time, a functional combination of the techniques is required. To prepare yourself for riding moguls, the following tasks and exercises are useful:

♦ turns with legs extended and increasingly narrower radii
♦ turns with legs extended, in terrain with changing inclination
♦ turns with legs extended and a high frequency of turns
♦ maintain rhythm when riding downhill trails
♦ travel terrains like wave pistes (gentle slope, low waves), low hilltops or tips, and compensate actively by flexing the legs (surfing the waves)
♦ from traversing, ride onto a hilltop and "swallow" it by flexing the legs
♦ practice equalization technique when riding onto a hilltop
♦ traverse in the moguls and "swallow" them by flexing the legs
♦ ride behind a partner in order to practice following a "pre-determined" riding line and rhythm

Exercises to practice and stabilize:

♦ ride on gentle mogul slope
♦ ride on mogul slope with low moguls
♦ ride only short sections (such as three moguls); later extend the length of the sections
♦ try to ride down a track line that you have pre-determined in your head;
♦ vary that pre-determined line
♦ pre-set own rhythm by voice or breathing
♦ accelerate your speed while riding moguls and then reduce it again

Tips:

♦ When riding moguls it is crucial to ride defensively and to have a track line in your head (at least for the first three turns) in order to be able to constantly adjust your technique to the terrain
♦ Mental preparation means to concentrate prior to the ride and mentally "ride down" the moguls
♦ For practice and training purposes, always ride down the same line to the extent possible
♦ As you ride, imagine that the legs are shock absorbers that compensate for all unevenness, and stay in contact with the

snow without the body itself moving up and down

◆ Maintaining a constant body tension makes controlling the board easier

◆ While riding, maintain a constantly low center of gravity and keep the body in a ready-to-move position

◆ Actively use both moguls and gaps when riding. Constantly working "against" the moguls is disruptive of a flawless, rhythmic ride

◆ Keep arms calm (moving them brings added unrest to the ride)

Safety:

Prior to the ride, your body has to be properly warmed-up and your thoughts focused on the upcoming ride. When you are physically or mentally tired, your ride should be postponed.

To be able to control your speed during the descent, avoid leaning too far back. Finally, if confronted with poor visibility, riding the moguls is not recommended.

Riding in Deep Powder

Riding in deep snow or powder is without a doubt one of the most exhilarating experiences a snowboarder can have. Gliding through and over the masses of snow is one of a snowboarder's greatest joys. The trouble of actually getting to a deep-snow slope is forgotten as soon as you make the first few turns and that rare feeling of freedom and ease overcomes you. To be the first to swing down a trackless, fresh snow slope is an almost indescribable expe-

rience, but one that every snowboarder can have after only a short period of practice. The reason for this is the relatively large surface of the snowboard. In deep snow, this surface gives the board a buoyancy that is not possible on any other winter-sport device. *Nevertheless, riding in deep powder is always risky.* Before going out to enjoy the "powder dream," you should get information on any avalanche warnings in the area, otherwise the dream can turn suddenly into a nightmare. Unfortunately, too, there are some reckless snowboarders who disregard all the dangers and warnings. Therefore, follow the lead of responsible snowboard instructors and use open slopes and trails only.

The basic technique for riding in deep powder closely follows the technical model of turns with legs extended and rhythmic stringing together of medium-long turns. For riding in deep snow, a certain set speed is required so that the board does not drown in the snow but "floats" up on top.

Technical model

The ride begins on the fall line in a relatively flexed position. By leaning into the turn, the weight is shifted onto the inside edge of the board and the legs are extended to adjust the board. In doing this, the body's center of gravity is shifted slightly to the back leg, which results in compressing the snow. At the end of the turn, the pressure on the compressed snow is slightly released by flexing the legs according to the compensation technique. At the same time as the legs are flexed, the body's center of gravity is tipped into the direction of the turn; as a result, the board is rolled onto the other edge. By gently giving-in to the

flexing when the board is rolled onto the other edge, the board starts floating up. As soon as the roll onto the other edge is completed, the next turn is initiated by extending the legs.

Notes and explanations

It is crucial to the turn radius that the extension is done in a controlled manner. By extending the legs in this way, the radii become wider; a fast extension of the legs results in an increased reduction in the size of the radii.

If the snow is not too deep, it is very possible to use the already familiar technical models of turning with the legs flexed or turning after pre-rotation. The problem with those techniques is that they have the tendency to "dig" the nose under the snow surface. But even using those techniques, the board will "swim up" in the snow if enough weight is shifted onto the back leg and the overall speed is faster. It is also possible, on a deep powder trail, to use all the other techniques learned so far.

Tasks and exercises:

To prepare for the first turns in deep snow, the following movement exercises are recommended:

◆ turns on the slope with legs extended

◆ turns with legs extended on the caterpillar's track on the freshly groomed slope

◆ the two exercises above but more rhythmically (e.g., at your own rhythm, pre-set by a partner riding ahead, or…)

◆ turns with legs extended with much/little leaning into the curve

◆ rides in deep powder on gentle terrain with a lot of run-out

◆ carefully, while gliding, trying different positions (leaning for-

ward/backward) to develop a sense for the right position

+ glide with strong up-and-down movements, feeling how the board sinks more into the snow when moving from a flexed to extended position

+ ride into the deep snow from the slope and carefully "play" with forward-backwards leaning

Further tasks and exercises:
Once turns on the slope are confidently mastered and you have gathered some first experiences in deep snow, focus on using and improving the various techniques in deep snow. To learn rhythmic turning in deep snow more quickly, start by practicing on non-prepared terrain. Furthermore, at this learning stage, it's recommended that you ride down only short stretches of the slope (just four to six turns) in order to strengthen the technique.

For this the following tasks and exercises are recommended:

+ turns upmountain in deep snow; descend in flexed position and rise to steer

+ in flat terrain, stay close to fall line and turn with legs extended

+ gain speed and repeat previous exercise

+ take increasingly wider turns

+ ride down a slope with changes in turn radii

+ vary above techniques in deep snow

Tips:
+ a certain overall speed makes it easier for the board to "swim" up

+ lean only slightly back; extreme leaning-back makes rolling the board onto the other edge more difficult

+ conduct all movements gently and smoothly; abrupt movements increase the danger of sinking into the snow

+ do not stop in gaps and hollows (skating in deep snow is *not* a pleasure)

+ in very steep terrain and at the beginning of the descent, wide turn radii and wide turn angles, respectively, are recommended in order to get a feel for the snow and to control speed

+ waste less energy on very long slopes by riding medium to wide radii

+ do not ride aimlessly down a slope, leaving fresh sections without tracks for the next ride (put tracks parallel to one another)

+ wide boards with little sidecut and a high nose and tail make swimming up in deep snow easier

+ consider moving binding slightly to the back

+ soft boots offer optimal freedom of movement in deep powder

Safety:
When riding in deep snow there is always a danger of avalanche. Therefore, never ride into a closed slope even if there are track marks there. Before a descent always get information on avalanche warnings for that particular slope from those knowledgeable (ski patrol). Furthermore, when riding in deep powder at least two snowboarders should always ride together, so that in case of an accident one can get help.

Riding in Steep Terrain

What is steep terrain, really? Does "steepness" begin at a 25 degree slope, or do you need a slope of 45 degrees or more to be called steep? Actually, it doesn't really matter how steep a slope is measured in degrees; steepness is always subjective, depending on how it is seen by the individual. Because of the fact that steepness is subject only to a person's own assessment, riding technique should always be adapted to individual conditions. Only by doing this can a rider master a slope.

The following applies to every rider: The board must cross the fall line quickly and every turn must be very effectively steered out to keep the speed controlled. Too, throughout the turn, attention must be paid to maintaining sufficient edge pressure and excellent body balance. If the slope is wide enough, the turn radii can be varied.

Technical model

The approach is taken in a flexed position to be able to relieve the load on the board by a rapid vertical movement. At the same time, the upper body and hip are pre-rotated in the direction of the turn and the entire body is put into a leaning position to prepare for turning the board and so the board rolls onto the other edge. At about the time the body is in open position to the downhill side, the torso turn is transmitted onto the board. The turn is controlled by flexing the legs in a smooth and restrained manner while continuing to rotate the torso a little bit farther in the direction of the turn. At the initiation of the turn, shift the weight onto the front foot and, during the course of the steering process, move it farther to the back.

Notes and explanations

In steep terrain the use of vertical movement and body rotation is

the key to a successful change of direction. The speed of the vertical movement determines how much and for how long for the board can be relieved. The extent of the rotation movement determines how fast the turn is and how wide its radius.

The steeper the terrain, the more dynamically the movements have to be carried out. For extreme passages, the jump turn, where the board lifts off the snow, is used. To do this requires a strong edging during steering so that you have enough edge-grip for the next turn. In order to edge, the knees are shifted more towards the mountainside and the body leans less into the turn. In very steep terrain, the right amount of movement is crucial for keeping control over the board.

Tasks and exercises to stabilize:
+ cut turns with distinct vertical movements
+ turns with narrow radii and wide angles
+ turns while holding hands on hips or in front of the body to control torso rotation and eliminate twisting of the spine

Tasks and exercises to vary:
+ turns with strong relief by upward movement (jump turns)
+ turns in differently inclined slopes
+ turns with changing radii/speeds

Tasks and exercises to practice:
+ turns in varied angles of steepness, with and without arm movement
+ turns over small bumps with immediate turn-initiation
+ jump turns in changing snow conditions

Tips:
In the beginning, the practice terrain used to establish and improve on technique should not be too steep. Fear is not a good teacher. Also, you should make sure to eliminate counter-rotation, when the board points in the direction of the turn and the torso in the exact opposite direction. This limits your ability to move, and makes it impossible to have sufficient control of the board. For the first few runs, choose short, steep slopes with sufficient runout. Always start with narrow radii, so as to be better able to control speed; later in the descent, you can enlarge the radii.

Safety:
When a chosen slope is too steep, sliding down the backside edge will allow you to check out any possible obstacles. Under no circumstances should you remove the board. The danger of uncontrolled slipping is much greater without the board attached.

Riding in Chutes

Chutes are among the most exciting terrain for snowboarders to travel. The character of this terrain is steep and narrow. Chutes are most often found in the high alpine parts of mountains, and they are, therefore, full of danger and risk.

Prior to entering a chute, you must be alert to any possible obstacles or hazards, like cliffs or sudden changes of direction. Such conditions will influence greatly the technique you should use.

In general, the following applies: The board has to be rotated across the fall line quickly and steered out immediately by putting the board on the edge with power.

Yet, it is important to steer out of every turn in a way that does not cause the board to gain speed that can subsequently result in a ride that is out-of-control.

Technical model
Prior to initiating the turn, ride a mountainside turn with controlled flexing. Follow it with a dynamic rise and simultaneous pre-rotation in the fall line to roll onto the other edge. Immediately thereafter, begin to steer out of the turn. In order to do this, you need to have your weight spread evenly on both legs. By changing the edge loads, you determine the amount of drift that you need to control your speed and initiate the next turn.

While arm movement plays an important role in maintaining balance, it is the edge work that is crucial for controlling your speed and line of travel. It's important that you roll quickly onto the other edge and edge *strongly*, so that the pressure on the edge is constantly increased.

Tasks and exercises to stabilize:
+ ride on medium-steep slopes with narrow radii and constant speed
+ same as above, but use strong vertical movements (called jump turns)
+ ride on steep slopes and use your imagination to set and ride narrow paths

Tasks and exercises to vary:
+ turns in steep terrain with determined arm movements
+ abruptly stop in middle of a flawless ride and start over
+ ride narrow radii by only pre-rotating

Tasks and exercises to stabilize:
+ ride on steep slopes with dif-

ferent types of snow

+ drift down steep slopes frontside and backside
+ ride 180° jump turns in steep terrain

Tips:

First rides should be made in relatively wide chutes in order for you to get used to the constricted slope conditions. Thoughtful and controlled entry into the chute is crucial so that you can apply the techniques you have learned so far into reality.

Soft boots allow the rider more flexibility in his or her movements. Unfortunately, especially on the back side, they offer clearly less support.

Safety:

Since chutes are mostly found in high alpine parts of mountains, it's important to choose the right route for the descent, as well as a safe route up.

Riding on Hard, Icy Snow

Hard and icy downhill trails create very difficult conditions for a snowboarder, because balancing on the board in a turn is often made more difficult by a sudden drifting of the board. To make matters even more difficult, the snow offers almost no resistance, so the board constantly moves faster and faster. Good control of the board by using the edges correctly and positioning the body perfectly are crucial to mastery in these conditions.

The most important criteria for controlling speed and track line is

the edge work. The rider must roll onto the other edge quickly, and edge more than usual so that the amount of pressure on the edge is increased.

Technical model

Approaching the first turn, the rider's knees must already be pointed towards the mountain in order to retain enough edge-grip for the coming actions. Rolling onto the other edge is done by a dynamic vertical movement (forward-up-downward) and a moderate pre-rotation so as to initiate steering immediately. The body leans into the turn just enough to ensure optimal edge pressure. Too much of a lean can cause the board to slip, and too little lean doesn't put the board on the edge enough.

The movements in the ankle, knee and hip joints are meant to absorb the entire movement and the unevenness in the slope. It is necessary to avoid over-rotating, otherwise putting the board flat on the snow will reduce the edge pressure.

At the initiation of the turn, the weight has to be over the front leg. During the course of the steering, the weight will be shifted more and more to the back.

Tasks and exercises to stabilize:

+ carved turns without pre-rotating and vertical movement
+ same as above, but with arms folded
+ same as above, but with differing radii

Tasks and exercises to vary:

+ carved turns with intense vertical movement
+ carved turns that are increasingly accelerated
+ turns with different amounts of leaning in the curves

Tasks and exercises to practice:

+ open/close carved turns at the end of turn
+ turns with distinct weight shifts forward/backwards
+ application of curve leaning and vertical movement with various distinctions

Tip:

An aggressive and dynamic riding style helps put more pressure on the edge. By practicing different curve radii you'll get a better feel for the edge and come up with a comfortable, individualistic riding style. Once you've developed confidence in your technique, you can increase the pressure by moving the back leg during the steering phase: for a backside turn move the back leg towards the front, and for a frontside turn push the back leg towards the back.

Safety:

If you ride in a distinctly compact, flexed position, the pain will be less severe should you take a fall. Too, it might be possible for you to get back up onto the board quickly afterward by propping yourself up with your arms.

Riding on Firm Snow

Due to the very different conditions of firm snow, riders need to deal with different rotation resistances. Technical skills play an important role here, but so do your choice of radii and speed. Since, in firm snow, there is usually enough space available, you can put these outside forces to good use.

Technical model

To adapt your technique to the changing rotation resistances, you will need to use various distinctive pre-rotations to initiate and steer the turn. The deeper the snow, the more intense pre-rotation needed. If there is not enough such rotation support, you will also need to perform a vertical movement to initiate and to steer the turn. The object of the vertical movement is to raise the board as far as possible out of the snow at the start of the turn and to put as little weight as possible on it during steering so the blade doesn't become buried in the snow. Your weight should be evenly distributed onto both legs but, as the depth of firm snow increases, the load can be shifted more towards the back. (As when riding in deep snow, a higher speed *lifts* the board higher off the snow, and allows you to reduce the scope of movement.) In firm snow, it's easier than in other types to master even steep terrain by just regulating speed and track line.

Tasks and exercises to stabilize:
+ turns on a medium-steep slope with pre-rotation
+ turns on medium-steep slope by switching load between front and back
+ turns with medium radii with controlled vertical movement

Tasks and exercises to vary:
+ turns with leaving weight on the back leg during the entire turn
+ drifted turns by exclusively leaning into the turn
+ turns with pre-rotation in different types of snow

Tasks and exercises to practice:
+ ride medium-steep, firm snow slopes with wide radii and controlled vertical movement
+ same as above, but without vertical movement
+ same as above, but with different turn radii

Tips:
It's recommended that you use a wider board (as when riding in deep powder) because the characteristics of the wider board's construction offer more buoyancy. In easier terrain, the technique can be varied to find out which is best used in firm snow.

Riding on firm snow is good practice for steeper slopes. The arms should be actively used for momentum and to stay balanced.

Riding on Crusted Snow and Pack-Snow

Crusted snow and pack-snow are among the most strenuous and insidious snow types. Uneven breaks in the covering can easily cause you to lose your balance and throw you off rhythm.

Technical model

The most effective technique is to start with an extreme dynamic rising movement, similar to the jump turn, coupled with a short and very intense turning of the body and a simultaneous rolling onto the other edge in the air. At the landing, the body has to be positioned in such a way that, immediately after landing, you can initiate the next turn. The radii have to be so short that there is only just enough time to stabilize. The more dynamic and powerful the ride and turns, the more rhythmic the ride will be.

Tasks and exercises to stabilize:
+ ride turns using a very strong vertical movement (up–forward––downward)
+ ride turns with a distinctive changing of the load
+ ride on the fall line, with jumps from tail to nose

Tasks and exercises to vary:
+ turning in medium-steep terrain with dynamic vertical movement
+ riding on a gentle mogul field with dynamic vertical movement
+ riding in medium steep terrain having different types of snow

Tasks and exercises to practice:
+ ride wide radii turns on flat terrain with pack-snow
+ try jump turns in medium-steep terrain with crusted snow

Tips:
While wide radii help to reduce power by outside forces during turns, they increase the risk of a fall. A wide board creates more buoyancy so is clearly better suited for riding outside marked slopes, especially in deep and crusted snow. The increased mobility of soft boots makes riding in difficult snow conditions easier.

Carving

Riding on the edge, also called carving, is especially spectacular! Quick turns with extreme curve leans are possible and fascinate both riders and observers alike. The typical characteristic is a precisely carved track with the shifted track marks clearly visible in the snow, resulting from the direct rolling onto the other edge without any drifts to the side.

Learning this technique requires a certain amount of feel, along with all the basics learned earlier in this book. In addition, your equipment plays a role that's not totally unimportant. Although carving is slightly easier on alpine-oriented boards fitted with plate bindings, it's possible to do it using all board types and bindings. Therefore, you should not attribute your carving success or failure wholly on your equipment.

Turns here are ridden exclusively on the edge. Sliding or drifting must be avoided completely. The direct move from edge to edge is made easier by continued relieving, alternatively rising and flexing, and comes into play much before the fall line, followed by cut turn steering.

Technical model

Approach by traversing with slightly flexed ankle, knee and hip joints. At turn initiation, the whole body moves forward-downward (rolling onto the other edge comes automatically), pressure is put against the inner edge, and the "appropriate" curve leaning position is assumed. The turn is initiated prior to the fall line. The turn is steered out by more edging (using foot and calf muscles) and a slight rotation of the torso in the direction of the turn.

Edge pressure, curve leaning and riding speed have to be consistent so that the board can "run" on the sidecut and open edge without drifting.

Notes and explanations

In the above technical model, the actions to be taken have not been strictly determined. This was done intentionally, because the amount of vertical movement is more or less useful depending on terrain, equipment and speed. The handling of the factors influencing the ride, as well as your own personal riding style, will ensure a "free usage" of the best vertical movement to be taken in any particular situation. The soft-boot rider tends to initiate the turn by a quick-flex relieving. The movement is almost invisible to the eye because it is primarily carried out only by the ankle joints. Steering, much more importantly, achieves its quality through the stance of the leg and foot muscles.

Very active soft-boot riders show this vertical movement, needed mainly for acceleration and during steering, distinctly. Hard boot riders, however, show the vertical ankle, knee and hip joints movements very distinctly because the main action is transferred to the upper "free" joints. For the alpine rider, an active vertical movement, due to the relatively static and heavy unit of board–binding–boot, is an important prerequisite for a fast roll onto the other edge and active drift-free steering.

The radius of the turns is determined by the sidecut of the board and the angle of the edge in the snow. This new dimension of steering the board merely by varying the edging angle requires intense concentration in practicing and correct methods.

Crucial for learning the technique of carving is an inner sense of movement, "letting the board run on edge (drift-free!)" and the control over the tracks. From the point of view of technique, the most suitable way to steer is in part the method described for turns with pre-rotation In the beginning, turns should be ridden irregularly. This will help you to get the necessary confidence for the rapidly increasing speed when carving cyclically. The perfect terrain for carving is a well-groomed and wide, gentle to medium-steep slope.

When the terrain is ideal—a gentle and open slope with plenty of run-out space—a completely rhythmic method of carving close to the fall line is recommended.

It's important to keep caution in mind here, even if you consider yourself a quite good beginning snowboarder. When you are gliding on the edge, even in flat terrain the board can reach very high speeds. If an edge should suddenly become jammed, it can cause a severe fall.

Tasks and exercises to carve by steering:

+ ride mountainside turns varying the edging angle
+ turn garlands (on a wide slope)
+ use an extended approach, steer out the turn by carving and continually controlled flexing
+ ride turns with hands on the hips to control hip rotation and omit twisting of the spine
+ carry something (knee pad, hat, scarf) in front of the body to control the rotation of the torso and flexing of the upper body

Tasks and exercises to carve by moving rhythmically:

+ gliding and edging practice close to the fall line

+ ride turns far out of the fall line
+ quick rolling onto the other edge close to the fall line
+ ride turns with extreme rising relief (jump turns)
+ link turns together with changing radii and speeds
+ ride turns without vertical movement
+ carved turns with rising to an acoustic rhythm pattern (down-up-up-up)
+ carving through vertical slalom course

Tips:

If you can't seem to let the board "run" on the edge, there could be various reasons which we will try to analyze separately here. It may be helpful to lower your speed, to increase the edging angle, to decrease the pre-rotation of the torso, to put more load on the tail of the board, or to ride in flat terrain.

If the board drifts during and immediately prior to and after rolling onto the other edge, you should try to move from edge to edge more quickly and to lean the entire body more forward-down the mountain, so as to increase speed at the turn initiation, to roll onto the other edge by leaning into the curve more before the fall line, and to decrease the pre-rotation but increase the body tension.

If the ride gets out of control by increasingly higher speed, the turns have to be steered out consciously and the board has to be put more on the edge. If the board jerks due to too much flexing of the hips and stiff legs, this can be remedied by flexing the ankle and knee joints, not by flexing or pre-rotating the upper body. If the torso rotates against the direction of the turn (counter-rotation), point the arms in the direction of the intended turn and move the eyes towards the turn.

Depending on the type of board and its intended use (symmetrical, asymmetrical; all-round, race or freestyle boards), a more or less shifting of the weight from the front to the back leg, or the other way around, is required. At a turn initiation more weight has to be put on the front leg, and towards the end of the turn on the back leg. The extent of the weight shift depends on many factors. Therefore, you will need to find out what is individually best for you. Even very good carvers constantly try to improve their technique by practicing on an ideal training slope under constant conditions to find the optimal trim for their board (binding angle and stance) and their best riding technique.

Racing

Racing is one of the special goals of snowboarding. Analyzing the guidelines coupled with the knowledge that you have previously gathered about snowboarding should enable you to draw conclusions on special technique characteristics that apply for snowboard racing.

The snowboarder who wants to succeed against competition between the gates doesn't need just a will to win, sponsors, and a fast board, but also a lot of experience and practice. In addition to specialized technical training, other general exercises to prepare you for riding between the gates need to be covered. They will prepare you not only to compete in race-specific situations, but also teach general skills that may be of use when riding on the open slope off the race course.

First, the snowboarder should be prepared for the limited room available for movement by using different training methods with a number of exercises. Only afterwards does it make sense to start practicing basic race technique.

Riding in confined spaces

By riding between the caterpillar tracks, for example, you are forced to adjust your radii and speed in accordance to the inclination of the slope. It is also possible to practice on gate courses, but this is a little bit excessive, as they must be mastered with different objectives. The exercises have different levels of difficulty depending on the design of the course.

Possible exercises:

+ ride turns within the marked course
+ ride as closely as possible to the gates
+ use the entire width of the course and maintain speed (from flat to steep terrain)
+ jump, rolling onto the other edge within the gate course (also jumping over markers)

Pre-set track

To follow another snowboarder's tracks exactly requires an ability to react quickly and ride with foresight. An even more exact binding to a track is provided by riding along gate fences.

Here, too, different exercises are possible:

+ ride along the outside
+ ride along the inside (only at poles)
+ alternate between riding inside and outside

Riding formation

Maintain a rhythmic movement. The rhythm you follow can be pre-determined from the outside by an instructor or music, or by a first rider (coach). This pre-setting is very similar to riding the gates.

Riding at high speeds

Attaining high speeds on the board is a must for the ambitious racer. A snowboarder has to get used to fast riding to be among the winners. But be careful! This is only possible when slope traffic and riding skills permit.

Basic racing technique

It doesn't matter if the course is a narrow dual slalom or a fast giant slalom, the objective is always the same:

Between the start and the finish there is a pre-set course that has to be mastered in the fastest possible time. The objectives "pre-set course" and "in the fastest possible time" are the basis for developing the basic racing technique. This basic racing technique is not a new way to ride turns. Rather, it is about the right timing and the specific use of the inner forces like muscles and body tension, as well as outside forces like centrifugal force, tension of the board and slope leeway forces. In coordination with the special features of racing, this technique has to be customized for each turn.

Crucial for fast riding between the gates are an understanding of the following facts:

+ gliding is faster than edging
+ edging is faster than drifting
+ a body reaches maximum speed if the body's center of gravity is as close as possible to the fall line
+ the movement of large body masses (the torso and arms)

away from the desired direction causes unrest and a disturbance in your balance

◆ rolling actively onto the other edge is possible only if there is solid ground underneath and the muscles are tensed. These pre-conditions are created by actively steering during the previous turn

To satisfy these facts during training, the individual aspects have to be selected, worked on and practiced separately, so that a complex and flawless basic racing technique can be developed.

To describe the basic racing technique, we will extract and cover here the most important movement phases: steering and rolling onto the other edge. Since these individual phases can hardly be separated during the ride, we can more easily describe some of the requirements needed for racing by combining the two phases.

Technical model

To make explaining the technique easier the steering phase, or riding on the edge, is divided into two parts — simply gliding on the edge and the short, dynamic move onto the edge (for added change of direction). The first part, gliding on the edge, starts immediately after rolling onto the other edge. Gliding on the edge means that the board is edged just enough not to drift, but carves into the turn. It cannot be edged more than needed or it will result in an increased brake-effect. The body is in a relatively extended position with the weight on the front foot. As soon as the board glides on the edge the snowboarder takes on a "waiting position." In this position, the rider has enough time to aim for the next gate.

Now to the second section: the

dynamic edging. In this part of the steering phase, the short, dynamic movement onto the edge, a flexing move over the back leg, is done to edge the board harder and, as a result, create high muscular tension. In addition, this flexing changes the travelling direction by narrowing the radius in such a way that, after rolling onto the other edge, the next gate can be aimed for more perfectly. By narrowing the radius the board is bent like a trampoline. The effect of this is that the tense body shoots up from the edge like a spring. The snowboarder should use this "rebound effect" to roll quickly onto the other edge.

While you are actually rolling onto the other edge, the board typically can't be steered, until you are again edging. Therefore, the snowboarder has to roll onto the other edge as quickly as possible to keep the loss of control to a minimum. The best technique to use to prepare for rolling onto the other edge comes from using the influences of outside forces like centrifugal force, speed and muscle tension, which arise at the end of the steering turn, and channeling them for the roll onto the other edge.

Further notes and explanations

When rolling onto the other edge, the body's center of gravity should, despite the rebound effect, remain at the same height above the snow. For that, the upper body should show little vertical movement over the board, in a straight line forward-downward. The board, however, runs or drives farther to the outside and subsequently is edged in an extended body position. The body's center of

gravity stays as close as possible to the fall line. The necessary forward-curve leaning at the beginning of the steering turn results from the radius that is pre-set by the course and from the speed. Your amount of lean has to be adjusted based on the inclination of the riding slope and the roughness/smoothness of the snow. The resulting basic racing technique coordinates with the special requirements of racing but, like all the technical models we've described, needs to be adjusted to the situation and special features of each turn. It is important to understand that the basic racing technique is not a permanent technical norm in itself, but a variation in dynamics, timing and amplitude of the "turns with legs flexed" technical model. The basic racing technique functions only as a guideline, to maximize your technical skills when riding on a pre-set course.

How to proceed

The elements of the basic racing technique can be divided into several individual movements of differing levels of difficulty which can then be "dry" practiced prior to riding the gate course. However, you must first be confident that you have learned the technical model given above, with carved-turn steering. Once the basics of this racing technique have been mastered, you can go on to practicing your racing technique with different radii, speeds and slope inclinations until you are, in effect, fit to compete.

Waiting position: Gliding on the edge in an extended body position requires you to change the timing of your customary movements. As an exercise, "intermission turns" are very useful. The rider takes a "break in moving" as soon as the board glides on the edge after rolling onto the other edge.

Exercise: "Jump on the ball of the front foot and stay there."

Forward-curve leaning: Forward- curve leaning depends on the inclination of the slope, radius and speed. These three factors change from turn to turn during a race. Therefore, in all terrain and riding situations you should experiment with your maximum forward-lean. Later, try different curve leanings until the feeling for the "right" amount of lean is found. It is the lean over the forward-curve at initiation of turn-steering that determines the curve radius.

Exercise: "Try to get your nose over the tip of the board."

Tip: Move forward-downward until the tail of the board breaks out or the tip starts to dig into the snow. Then, retract a little so that the board glides on the whole length of the edge after rolling onto the other edge.

Rolling onto the other edge: In racing, the roll onto the other edge is not done by rising over the front leg, as in the technical model, but rather by a rising motion directly forward-downward. The distance of the body's center of gravity "over above" the board is clearly reduced, which results in a faster roll onto the other edge.

Vertical movement: The precise flexing movement at the end of the steering phase is mounted on the previous overall movement. Additional supporting means are useful to work out correct timing.

Exercise: "At the gate, try to bring your weight to the lowest possible position over the back foot."

The selection of the riding track

is crucial for an effective use of the basic racing technique. The gates are approached "high," if possible. This means the rolling onto the other edge has to be completed as soon as possible after the last gate. If you would divide the distance between two gates into three even parts, the board has to be rolled onto the other edge at the end of the first third. The next gate can be approached, in a relatively straight line in waiting position, over the next two thirds.

Quick rolling onto the other edge: First, you have to adjust your feel for rolling onto the other edge instantly, and it should include the rebound effect for the roll. This demands the highest technical skill. In the shortest possible time, all occurring forces must be channeled to achieve the following.

✦ the body's center of gravity remains at the same level of height above the snow
✦ the move from edge to edge is completed as fast as possible
✦ the body's center of gravity remains as close as possible to the fall line
✦ after rolling onto the other edge the body is in an extended position with the weight over the front foot, and
✦ the edging angle to the snow is wide enough that the board glides on the edge with as little as possible brake-effect

Tips for practice planning:
✦ snowboard as often as possible
✦ ride as many different terrains as possible, including moguls and deep powder to practice a variable readiness of techniques
✦ at every opportunity and terrain practice individual elements of the basic racing technique

✦ at each set slalom course ask for permission to ride it and get accustomed to the gates
✦ as soon as the elements are worked out, practice and improve the overall movement patterns in different terrain
✦ towards season's end, intense technical training in the gates
✦ during the summer, extensive stamina and physical-strength training by mountain biking or inline skating
✦ at the beginning of the season, practice fast but safe riding
✦ repeat and improve technical elements
✦ afterwards, implement race technique, strength and speed on a race course

Freestyle

In this chapter you will learn about freestyle snowboarding. But can freestyle be defined? Halfpipe, quarterpipe, big airs, slope tricks, riding fakie, carving… all are a part of freestyle but they cannot actually be placed in the same category.

When you ride freestyle, you allow your creativity to run free. By bringing your own own individual style into the technique, your enjoyment of snowboarding is increased. Freestyle is the perfect way to add to your snowboarding fun and make it even more versatile, through incorporating your own personal style. In this sense, the following chapter offers a few "fun enhancers" as suggestions.

Equipment

Constantly changing developments in snowboards, bindings and boots, and the availability of the products in various areas make it almost impossible to provide perfect recommendations for freestyle equipment. Therefore, the following information is necessarily limited to currently up-to-date freestyle equipment and to a brief overview of their respective areas of use.

Boards

The length of the freestyle board depends on both the size of the rider and the intended area of use. In general, lightweight riders ride rather shorter boards and heavier riders longer boards. Moreover, longer boards are very well-suited for free-riding off-slope due to their good buoyancy, but are a little sluggish for doing tricks and jumps. Shorter boards are generally easier to rotate and therefore excellent to use as "pure freestyle boards." Due to their poor buoyancy, however, they are not suited for free-riding off-slope.

The width of the board is responsible for the maneuverability and readiness to turn; for free-riding, it is usually pre-determined by your shoe size. Binding angle, shoe size and riding style determine the minimum width of the board.

For freestyle boards as well as other types, the sidecut plays an important role. Boards with little sidecut are good for drifting and are more forgiving of mistakes at slope tricks. For free-riders and advanced freestylers, boards with more sidecut are recommended since they have a broader area of use.

The upward bends of nose and tail can be characterized as follows:

A long and flat nose offers good buoyancy in deep snow, but is in the way when doing tricks due to its great mass. Therefore, long and flat noses are mostly found on free-ride boards. A short nose is recommended for "exclusively freestyle boards" because of its small mass. Upward bends of the tail are mostly good for fakie tricks.

Bindings

Conventional freestyle bindings mostly consist of a base, two straps and a high back. In contrast to a conventional free-ride binding, it offers more mobility to the sides. Some free-ride bindings have three straps for better support. It is very important to have good heel support; moreover, straps and high backs should be padded.

The latest in binding developments are step-in bindings. There is a difference between free-ride step-in systems and freestyle step-in systems. In free-ride step-in systems, the high back is usually integrated into the boot. The binding itself is just a flat plate with a fastening mechanism. If the integrated high back is designed to be flexible to the side (e.g., by a joint), the system is more or less suited for freestyle. The step-in systems designed purely for freestyle riding consist of a "normal" freestyle boot with a binding adapter integrated in the sole and a binding with high back.

Mounting angle/stance width:
Positioning the bindings for your individual needs and tastes involves a lot of experimenting. Riders usually use a stance width of about 24 inches (60 cm) and a binding angle of 0°/0°, or even a duck stance (negative back angle). Recently, the trend has been to move away from very extreme binding positions—even in the half pipe, a binding angle of 35° in the front is used. Following is an overview of the range of binding positions that are normal for freestyle snowboarding. Based on the figures following, it is up to each rider to find the optimal position for him- or herself.

Mounting angle front: 0° to 35°
Mounting angle back: -10° to 15°
Binding stance width: 18 to 24 inches (45–60 cm)

Regarding binding placement on the board, generally a central position is very well-suited for tricks, jumps and riding fakie; but this positioning is not the best for deep snow and for free-riding on the slopes. For free-riding, bindings should be mounted about an inch (2 to 3 cm) behind the sidecut center; for deep-snow riding, even up to 2 inches (6 cm) behind the sidecut center.

Basic riding technique

Riding fakie

Riding fakie is, on the one hand, a new challenge to improve your riding skills and, on the other hand, a necessity for various tricks (rotation jumps, half pipe, etc.).

Riding fakie is actually no different from riding backwards. The ready position is unchanged, only the head is turned into the new riding direction.

The problem in riding fakie is not in the riding technique itself (it's identical to riding forward), but in your own mind. It means briefly having to relearn snowboarding again, from the beginning. The first question that invariably arises is "How do I get *into* the fakie riding position?" There are numerous ways to get into this backwards position.

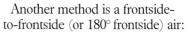

Another method is a frontside-to-frontside (or 180° frontside) air:
- ✦ during the frontside-fakie ride, flex legs to prepare for the jump
- ✦ jump off the mountainside edge by extending legs while simultaneously rotating towards down-mountain
- ✦ continue rotating in the air — the head points in the direction of the rotation at all times — and prepare for landing on the new mountainside edge
- ✦ land fakie on the new frontside edge, flexing at the same time to absorb the landing, then steer out the turn until completed

(Other ways to get into the fakie riding position are the noseroll 180° or the ollie 180°, which will be described later.)

Perhaps the easiest is simply the over-rotation of a backside turn, which is done as follows:
- ✦ over-rotate the backside turn until the board stops
- ✦ shift weight onto the new front leg and continue riding in fakie

Possible exercises in gentle to medium-steep terrain:
- ✦ side sliding with alternating weight shifts on the front and back legs
- ✦ traversing fakie
- ✦ start normally, but rotate from a turn into fakie position

Wheelie

Wheelie is riding with either only the tail (tailwheelie) or only the nose (nosewheelie) touching the snow. This maneuver is done by an extreme shifting of the rider's weight along the length axis of the board.

Tailwheelie

Nosewheelie

Waltz

The waltz is a 360° rotation of the board on a slope. It can be used as an exercise to ride fakie, but it can also be a maneuver of its own. Medium-steep terrain is the perfect terrain for practicing.

✦ Riding the approach to the fall line, a strong forward rotation is carried out. The board follows the rotation and is rolled onto the other edge near the fall line.

✦ Continue the rotation while simultaneously shifting the weight onto the front leg, until the nose points toward the mountain.

✦ Continue rotating while simultaneously shifting the weight onto the back leg. The board follows the rotation of the torso (and is again rolled onto the other edge near the fall line).

Ollie

The ollie maneuver comes from skateboarding enthusiasts and is the basis for the jumping technique. It is a way of taking off without using a ski jump; that is, the take-off is carried out without terrain support by using your own strength and technical skills. A flat terrain with perhaps gentle waves is best for practicing the following:

+ approach in flexed position
+ shift weight slightly towards the back while simultaneously pulling up the front leg
+ push away powerfully with back leg (extension)
+ draw legs up
+ stretch the legs slightly in preparation for landing
+ flex knees to absorb landing

Riding variations and combo techniques

By using your own creativity and individuality any number of variations and combinations can be put together utilizing the "basics." The following examples provide only a small spectrum of what it is possible for you to do on the snowboard, using soft boots. There's actually no limit to the imagination here.

Noseroll 180°

The noseroll 180° is a rotation on the nose of the board around 180° while gliding. It is another way to get into a fakie riding position.

+ approach on the fall line, move weight onto the front leg
+ backside rotation, weight remains on front leg
+ conclude rotation, shift weight back onto both legs and ride fakie

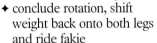

Noseroll 360°

The movements for the noseroll 360° are mainly the same as for the noseroll 180°. The difficult part, in comparison to the noseroll 180°, is the over-rotation over the fall line. It's extremely important here to keep the weight constantly on the front leg and to continue to rotate the upper body!

+ from traversing backside, rotate with a simultaneous shifting of the weight onto the front leg
+ keep the weight constantly on the front leg during the crucial over-rotation over the fall line
+ continue rotating on the nose then slowly shift weight onto both legs

Ollie grab

Jumping without a ski jump, as when doing an ollie, is not too much of a problem once it's learned, but if you spice the whole thing up with a grab, it really adds to the fun. Simply, while jumping you try to grab the board with one hand.

Ollie 180°

The ollie 180° is a jump with a 180° rotation of the board, offering another way to get into the fakie riding position. It is surely not the easiest way, but it is a very nice one for rider and observer alike!
+ the take-off is like the standard ollie, but with the upper body already slightly twisted
+ continue rotating in the air; the head turns too
+ make a soft landing

Ollie 180° to nosewheelie to tailroll 180°

This sequence is not really one individual trick but a "three-in-one." An ollie 180° is landed on the nose; after the wheelie, the board is "rolled" 180° on its tail.

Carve-grab

Carve-grab is carving while grabbing the outside edge of the board. This riding skill demonstrates the close relationship between snowboarding and surfing the waves.

Crucial to the carve-grab is the extremely low position – which makes the grab possible – and an even distribution of your weight onto both legs. Warning: Despite all the "style," it's important to *let go* of the board's edge in time!

Carving fakie

Carving fakie is the natural heightening of the experience of riding fakie. It is extremely important that only the head be pointed in the travelling direction while the rest of the body remains in ready position!

Slide

Like the carve-grab, the slide also demonstrates a close relationship to surfing. Instead of the surfer's "lip," however, for the slide you need a raised edge on the slope, a natural edge, or an embankment (whatever you could use to slide).

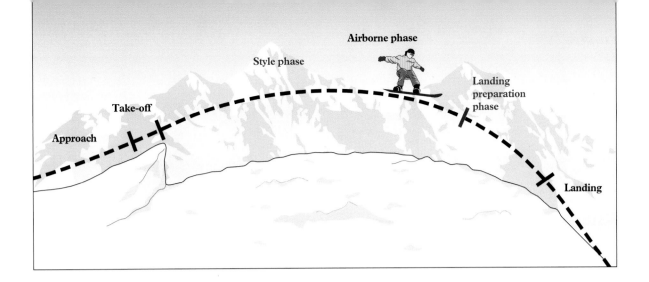

Basic jumping technique

Ollie and standard jump

Prior to discussing the jumps, it makes sense to explain the individual phases of a jump in detail.

to the take-off platform of the ski jump (quarter- and half-pipes are exceptions)

Airborne phase

✦ after take-off, take on a compact and smaller position

Landing

✦ controlled flexing
✦ distribute weight evenly onto both legs (when landing in deep snow the weight has to be moved a little bit towards the back)

As a general rule, the landing hill should never be too flat.

Approach
✦ "see" jump exactly and clearly
✦ take lower position at approach
✦ focus eyes on the take-off point

Take-off (active)
✦ "controlled" extending of ankle, knee and hip joints (not a complete extension)
✦ if possible move arms forward to gain momentum
✦ load weight evenly onto both legs; take-off is always vertical

✦ the airborne phase consists of the style phase and the landing preparation phase. During the style phase, the snowboarder can flip, rotate, grab…any style he or she likes. During the landing preparation phase, the maneuver or rotation has to be dissolved or completed
✦ in landing preparation phase, the legs must again be slightly extended (to perform their shock-absorbing function)

Mute grab: Front hand on frontside edge

Setting your style

"What am I supposed to do while I'm in the air?" The time for snowboarders to ask themselves this question is before take-off, not while flying! Everything that can be done in the air is an element of style. Some style maneuvers are more popular; and others are not. Regardless of the suggestions given here, the important thing is that the person doing "the flying" has to *like* doing it, and has to have a good feeling while doing it, because it's only then that the flight elements become "your" style. For example, you could grab the board, could perform contortions, flex and bend yourself, stretch a leg out, etc.

The variety of style elements can make it difficult to decide, but you should know, before starting the approach, which figure you want to execute. Therefore: Don't try everything at once! Slowly feel your way and test out elements of the many different styles. Only after you are able to perform the individual parts satisfactorily should you combine them one with one another for an individualized style.

Backside nosebone: Front hand grabs backside edge, front leg is extended

Stylized jump techniques

The variety of jumps has (almost) no limit. Based on the standard jump, there are countless variations and combinations created by different kinds of grabs, bones, tweaks and rotations in every direction. The demonstration of every such jump would certainly go beyond the scope of this book. Therefore, we present only a few of the more popular jump styles.

Standard jump with frontside grab

For the frontside grab, the grabbing of the board is added to the normal movement pattern of the standard jump. To do this, it's important to take on a flexed position during the airborne phase and grab the frontside edge in between the bindings with the back hand.

Frontside nosebone

The frontside grab can be expanded by boning — extending the front leg and simultaneously flexing the back leg.

Tweaked frontside nosebone

The tweaked frontside nosebone is even more complicated. In addition to grabbing and boning, the upper body is rotated. For that, the board is boned at an angle to the front (in frontside direction), and the front leg is stretched to the side. The upper body turns slightly in the opposite direction to even out the movement of the board. (The legs rotate against the upper body.) For landing, the tension of the body is released again.

Shifty

When doing the shifty, the legs are twisted against the upper body. This causes significant body tension which is not resolved until the landing preparation phase. The front leg is stretched out powerfully to the side, while at the same time the upper body is rotated to the other side. Front hand and front leg each point in different directions.

Backside air

The backside air surely is one of the oldest and best-known jumps in snowboarding. It is a classic!

With the front hand, you grab the backside edge. It's up to each snowboarder to decide if he or she grabs the board in-between the bindings, more towards the nose, or exactly by the front binding (as shown in the photo here). The front leg is bent and the back leg is pushed sideways towards the front. The board then lies in the air, with the bottom of the board pointing in the flying direction. The upper body is slightly rotated in the flying direction to balance out the system. The back hand is also extended to the front so that the movement of the board can be evened out. A great arc of tension like this can give the jump a stunning individual style.

180° and 360°

How about a whole rotation in the air? A learning tip: start first with a 180° practiced on a small embankment. The advantage is that you can practice the jump "in place" so to speak, meaning that less speed is required and the danger of injury is less.

Prior to take-off, draw back the arms to gain momentum.

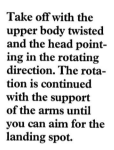

Take off with the upper body twisted and the head pointing in the rotating direction. The rotation is continued with the support of the arms until you can aim for the landing spot.

Bend knees for landing

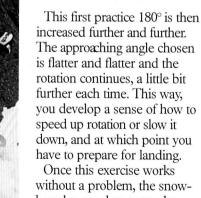

This first practice 180° is then increased further and further. The approaching angle chosen is flatter and flatter and the rotation continues, a little bit further each time. This way, you develop a sense of how to speed up rotation or slow it down, and at which point you have to prepare for landing.

Once this exercise works without a problem, the snowboarder can dare to try the jump at a real ski jump and enjoy the full, all-around view while flying. The following, however, has to be observed:

+ as early as take-off, the upper body, arms and head are pre-rotated in the desired direction
+ continue this rotation during the jump
+ when the landing spot is located, stop the rotation by not rotating the head, upper body and arms forward or further anymore
+ shortly before landing, the legs are stretched out again to better absorb the impact
+ bend the knees for landing

These few tips may have served to demonstrate that there are countless variations and combinations. And after all, it is also possible to do jumps "switch stance"— which means a goofy rider jumps as if he were a regular rider and others the other way around. Some snowboarders improve the technique and level of difficulty of their jumps, others just try to jump farther, higher and "more stylishly" through the air. Regardless of what and how you do it, the most important thing is that you have fun snowboarding.

Types of ski jumps

Naturally, the type of ski jump is not an entirely unimportant point when jumping. Not all ski jumps are alike.

Actually, there are three types, and because each type of ski jump calls for a slightly different technique, this section will describe these different types and the technique elements that go with each.

Flat ski jump/edge

Characteristic of ski jump

Flat take-off angle, flat take-off platform, no compression in approach; consequently, it follows that there is a light take-off and a flat, partially dropping flight path.

Take-off training
Swallowing or slowly riding over the ski jump, slightly increase speed and let yourself sail off (passive take-off); later increase speed for an active take-off.

Steep ski jump

Characteristic of ski jump
Steep take-off angle, compression in approach, which causes the take-off to be more difficult; flight path ascending—turning point—descending; the turning point is ideal for holding figures.

Take-off training
Swallowing or slowly riding over the ski jump, slightly increase speed and let yourself sail off (passive take-off), increase speed for an active take-off.

Quarter halfpipe

Characteristic of ski jump
Vertical take-off angle, vertical flight path; ascending—turning point—descending; landing in the vertical.

Take-off training
Ride without taking off (turn), passive take-off (let yourself "sail off"), active take-off in upward direction of intended flight path (different from normal take-off!). If the wall is not entirely vertical, the take-off must be corrected accordingly.

Index